Environmentalism

A Global History

Environmentalism

A Global History

RAMACHANDRA GUHA

 LONGMAN

An Imprint of Addison Wesley Longman, Inc.

New York • Reading, Massachusetts • Menlo Park, California • Harlow, England
Don Mills, Ontario • Sydney • Mexico City • Madrid • Amsterdam

Editor in Chief: Priscilla McGeehon
Executive Marketing Manager: Sue Westmoreland
Project Manager: Dora Rizzuto
Design Manager and Cover Designer: Wendy A. Fredericks
Cover Photo: © Artville
Senior Print Buyer: Hugh Crawford
Page Makeup: Guru Typograph Technology

Please visit our website at http://www.awlonline.com

ISBN 0-321-01169-4

for
Bill Burch, internationalist

Series Editor's Preface

Of the several processes that all human societies in all ages have had in common, none has been more fundamental than their continual interaction with their natural environment. In fact, more than any other aspect of human endeavor, the diverse modes of human societal interaction with the larger ecological setting provide the basis for a genuinely global history of humanity. But, unlike so many of the other themes and patterns from which world history can be constructed, environmental history transcends the human experience. Due to the profound technological and scientific transformations that have occurred over the past millennium, it has come to effect—often fatally in recent centuries—every species of living creature on earth.

In view of its centrality, it is rather remarkable that serious work on the global dimensions of the history of human responses to and impact upon their environments has, with important exceptions, been undertaken only in the last three or four decades. There were, of course, important ecological dimensions to the patterns of societal development that Ibn Khaldun delineated in his fourteenth-century treatise *The Muqaddimah*, especially in his stress on the ebb and flow of pastoral nomadic and sedentary adaptations in the history of North Africa and the Middle East. And George Perkins Marsh's magisterial meditation on *Man and Nature* was published nearly a century and a half ago. But it is only since the 1960s, that world and cross-cultural historians, led by William H. McNeill, Alfred Crosby, and more recently John McNeill, have embarked on sustained and thoroughly documented explorations of the diverse patterns of social and environmental interactions over time.

Thus far, much of the research and writing that these pioneering historians have inspired has been focused on specific ecosystems or regional complexes of environmental patterns. And almost all of the work done thus far, including that of more globally-oriented pioneers like McNeill and Crosby, has concentrated on actual processes of human interventions into the natural world and their consequences for both human societies and affected plant and animal species. Though a considerable amount has been written on the attitudes

towards the natural world exhibited by specific cultures or civilizations, little work has yet appeared that attempts to study these cross-
culturally or from a global perspective. The most important exception
to this general trend is Clarence Glacken's massive *Traces on the Rhod-
ian Shore*, which surveys responses to the environment from ancient
times to the modern era. But Glacken's work is oriented to European
thinkers and civilizations and to the ancient Mediterranean milieux
that give rise to them.

Given this situation, Ramachandra Guha's *Environmentalism: A
Global History* is an especially welcome addition to the Longman
World History series. Guha's incisive and wide-ranging survey of environmental thinking and the movements it has spawned is genuinely cross-cultural and global in scope. His focus is environmentalism
in the modern age, but he delineates and explores in depth a multipli-
city of approaches to those issues, with particular emphasis on the
often variant currents of the latter half of the twentieth century. Ideas
about the environment and movements aimed at focussing attention
on the causes of its degradation and the ways to protect it are set in
the different socioeconomic and political contexts which gave rise to
them. But Guha is also sensitive to the ways in which thinking about
ecology is reworked or transformed when it is exposed to international
or intercultural influences. He seeks to identify the commonalities
and differences in environmental thinking and activism through case
studies drawn from the experience of areas as diverse as the United
States, the former Soviet Union, China, India, Africa and Brazil. Guha
candidly assesses the strengths and shortcomings of each of these
strands of environmentalism as well as their contributions to the coale-
scence of a global environmental consciousness.

In many ways Ramachandra Guha is the ideal person to author
the first genuinely global history of environmentalism. Over the past
two decades, his many fine books and articles have earned him the
reputation as one of the foremost thinkers on ecological issues relating
to South Asia, historically one of the pivotal regions in environmental
history for reasons he elucidates in the study that follows. In recent
years, building on his regional expertise, Guha has become one of
the more provocative and perceptive commentators on environmentalism in its cross-cultural and global dimensions. He has made a
convincing case for the importance of understanding the often fundamental differences that separate Euro-American environmental activists and theorists and those who argue from the perspective of the
post-colonial societies, where the great majority of humanity lives.
He has placed great emphasis on the critical distinctions between

strains of ecological activism based on preservationist, conservationist, earth first, and human accomodationist priorities. His capacity to identify and analyze the central precepts of these different strands of environmentalism, in combination with his well-informed critiques of each of them in the larger context of the current global predicament, render *Environmentalism: A Global History* a lively and engaging study of ideas and debates that all of us will find central to our lives in the twenty-first century.

MICHAEL ADAS
Series Editor
Rutgers University at New Brunswick

Author's Preface

The roots of this book go back to two gloriously happy years I spent working at Yale University in the mid 1980s. On the basis of my own work in India I had imagined environmentalism to be principally a question of social justice, of allowing the poor to have as much claim on the fruits of nature as the powerful. But living and teaching in the United States I was to come face-to-face with a rather different kind of environmentalism, which shifted attention away from humans towards the rights of plants, animals and wild habitats. I have ever since been fascinated by the diversity within the global environmental movement. This book explores the part played by different cultural and national traditions in the making and shaping of that diversity.

I returned to India from the USA in 1987, but have gone back several times since, to renew acquaintance with and deepen my understanding of American environmentalism. More recently, I spent the academic year 1994–95 in Germany, a country that is unquestionably the leader within Europe in matters environmental, and is home also to the German Greens, the protest movement which became a political party. Briefer trips to Latin America in 1994, to Russia in 1996, and to Southern Africa in 1997, allowed a glimpse of the problems and possibilities of environmentalism in those territories.

These forays, short and long, have been paid for by hospitable universities and indulgent foundations who have helped me challenge one of the unacknowledged taboos of international scholarship. For the way that the world is structured, Brazilians may write about Brazil, Nigerians about Nigeria, Bangladeshis about Bangladesh. But broader works of contrast and comparison, books that are not restricted to one country but which take the world as their oyster, are written from the comfortable citadels of a great and prosperous university in Europe or the United States. This prejudice is not cultural or racial, but merely geographical. Global histories, be they of environmentalism, feminism, liberalism or fundamentalism, are generally the handiwork of people working and teaching in the northern half of the globe. It is as difficult for a scholar of British origin to write a global history living in Bogota as it is easy for an Indian while based in Indianapolis.

My thanks then, first of all, to the School of Forestry and Environmental Studies at Yale University. Two colleagues at Yale, Bill Burch and Joe Miller, and two students, Mike Bell and Joel Seton, encouraged me to move beyond what had been, until then, a near-obsessive concern with the history and politics of my own country. Next in chronological order comes the University of California at Santa Barbara, whose invitation in 1989 to deliver the Ninth Steven Manley Memorial Lecture forced me to think more seriously about the comparative aspects of the environmental question. The arguments of that lecture were given a firmer empirical basis in the year I spent at the Wissenschaftskolleg zu Berlin, whose magnificently efficient library staff chased and procured dozens of obscure references and out-of-print books. Other institutions that have helped materially include the University of California at Berkeley; the Harry and Frank Guggenheim Foundation, New York; the Social Science Research Council, New York; and the Nehru Memorial Museum and Library, New Delhi: my thanks to all of them.

The themes and arguments of this book have been shaped by numerous conversations across the continents. I have learnt much from three scholars whose interests exemplify the cross-cultural character of the environmental movement: from Juan Martinez-Alier, a Spaniard most at home in Ecuador and Cuba; from Mike Bell, a Rhode Islander who happily mixes with Little Englanders; and from Wolfgang Sachs, a Bavarian radical with a keenly developed insight into the practice of the Gujarati Mahatma, Gandhi. There are other friends in Europe and American with whom I have argued fiercely or gently but always (to me, at any rate) productively, and yet others who have passed on valuable tips and sources. I thank here William Beinart, David Brokensha, J. Peter Brosius, Louise Fortmann, Andrew Hurrell, Arné Kalland, Margit Mayer, Arné Naess, Paul Richards, David Rothenberg, Katherine Snyder, Carol Warren and Donald Worster. I owe a particular debt to K. Sivaramakrishnan (of Yale, again), the source of a steady stream of books and articles impossible to get hold of in India.

To come home now, to the students and scholars of the Indian environmental movement, the college of colleagues to whom I perhaps owe most of all. Discussions over many years with Anjan Ghosh, Madhav Gadgil and Shiv Visvanathan have helped me more clearly see India in the cold light of the world, and the world through the warm glow of India. I have also been challenged and inspired by the

verse and zest of younger colleagues such as Amita Baviskar, Ashish
Kothari, Mahesh Rangarajan and Nandini Sundar. André Béteille, a
distinguished senior scholar, and Keshav Desiraju, an experienc-
ed environmental administrator, read and helpfully commented on
an earlier draft. For valuable comments on the manuscript I am in-
debted to the following reviewers: Randall Dodgen (Sonoma State
University); Robert Entenmann (St. Olaf College); Vera Reben (Ship-
pensburg University); Cathy Skidmore-Hess (Georgia Southern University); Tracey Steele (Sam Houston State University). I would also
to thank my editors, Pam Gordon at Addison Wesley Longman (New
York) and Rukun Advani at Oxford University Press (New Delhi)
for their critical support to the project.

But it is, of course, the editor of this series who made the book
possible, who gently nudged all that talking and listening towards
the more reliable medium of print. Michael Adas invited me to write
on global environmentalism, waited trustingly as I missed one dead-
line after another, and then, when the draft chapters finally began to
arrive, sent them back with meticulously detailed comments. It is a
pleasure to thank him for all this, and a delight to remember those
happy days at Yale when Michael and I first met.

Contents

1

Going Green

The environmental movement is a child of the sixties that has stayed its course. Where other manifestations of that decade of protest—pacifism, the counter-culture and the civil rights struggle—have either lost out or lost their way, the green wave shows no sign of abating. The environmental movement has refused to go away and, some would say, refused to grow up, retaining the vigor and intensity but also the impatience and intolerance of an ever-youthful social movement. Alone among the movements of the sixties, it has gained steadily in power, prestige and, what is perhaps most important, public appeal.

Popular support apart, the success of the environmental movement is also reflected in the forests and wild areas it has helped set aside, as well as in the laws it has repealed or got enacted, nowhere more effectively than in the United States of America. In this country the pressures of environmentalists, rather than autonomous government action, have created an extensive and for the most part well managed system of national parks. Having protected large chunks of wilderness from the threat of 'development,' the American environmental movement has increasingly turned its attention to controlling the hazardous byproducts of industrialization: air and water pollution, and the production of toxic or radioactive wastes. Here too it has been conspicuously successful, forcing Congress to enact over seventy environmental measures into law. Among these is the National Environment Protection Act of 1969, a comprehensive piece of legislation and the envy of environmentalists in other countries who struggle to enforce minimum standards on their own governments.

While opinion polls consistently show over two-thirds of the public in support of even stricter environmental measures—and willing to part with some hard-earned dollars in the cause—the green agenda is also influencing the outcome of local, state and federal elections. Politicians from both parties assiduously project a green image and cultivate a green constituency. It was a Republican President, George Bush, who famously remarked, 'We are all environmentalists now.' The Democrats, not to be outdone, sent forth as Vice-President the author (Al Gore) of a respectably thorough and best-selling survey of the environmental dilemma, entitled *Earth in the Balance*. As the politicial scientist Richard Andrews points out, the influence of the environmental movement is 'demonstrable in all levels of government in extraordinary quantities of legislation, regulations and budgetary allocations, as well as in continuing media attention.' Or as John Oakes, an editor at the *New York Times*, writes of the movement's most cherished achievement, 'The national parks are as sacred to most Americans as the flag, motherhood and apple pie.'

Like apple pie, but unlike the flag, national parks are distinctively but not uniquely American. For the beauty and diversity of its resident species and habitats, Serengeti in Tanzania is probably more celebrated than Yellowstone in Wyoming, Manas in eastern India at least as remarkable as Yosemite in California. Indeed, environmentalism is by now a genuinely international movement, occurring with lesser or greater intensity in a variety of countries around the globe. Nor do these national movements necessarily work in isolation. In the age of e-mail and the fax machine, information generated in one country can be instantaneously transmitted to another. Environmentalism has thus come to constitute a field-of-force in which different individuals and organizations, far removed in space, collaborate and sometimes compete in forging a movement that often transcends national boundaries.

II

Moving outwards from the American experience, this book presents a global history of the environmental movement. Its focus is not on the nature and extent of environmental degradation; thus it has little to say about the rates of tropical deforestation, the extinction of species, or the build-up of carbon in the atmosphere. Those facts are properly the preserve of the scientist. Rather, this is a historical account and analysis of the origins and expressions of environmental concern, of how individuals and institutions have perceived, propagated, and acted upon their experience of environmental decay. This is a book, in sum, of the environment as a spur to human reflection and human action, rather than a scientific study of the state of nature or a balance sheet of the impact of human beings on the earth.

As a program of political reform, articulating concrete policies for states and societies to adopt, environmentalism needs to be distinguished from a more narrow aesthetic or scientific appreciation of the natural world. Classical literary traditions manifest an abiding concern with natural landscapes: in writing of the beauty of birds, animals, rivers and farms, both the Roman poet Virgil (c. 70–1 BC) and the Sanskrit dramatist Kalidasa (c. AD 375–415) would qualify as 'nature-lovers'. Moving on to the late Middle Ages, the exploration by European travellers of Asia and the Americas also kindled a keen interest in the richness and diversity of nature. The exuberance of plant and animal life in the tropics was documented by a whole array of European scientists, of whom the Englishman Charles Darwin (1809–82) is perhaps the best known and most influential.

However, as understood in this book environmentalism goes beyond the literary appreciation of landscapes and the scientific analysis of species. I argue that environmentalism must be viewed as a *social* program, a charter of action which seeks to protect cherished habitats, protest against their degradation, and prescribe less destructive technologies and lifestyles. When then did the environmental movement begin? Most accounts of the American movement date its beginnings to Rachel Carson's book on pesticide pollution, *Silent Spring*, published in 1962 and variously described as the 'bible' and 'founding event' of modern environmentalism. It is true that it is only in the sixties that environmentalism emerges as a popular *movement*, successfully influencing public policy through a mixture of protest in the streets and the lobbying of legislators in the corridors of power. However, an intellectual concern for the protection or conservation of nature goes back at least to the last decades of the eighteenth century. This precocious interest rapidly grew in the nineteenth century, its votaries seeking to influence the modernizing governments of North America and Europe. Without always commanding a mass base, this earlier generation of environmentalists initiated wideranging programs of forest and water conservation and also helped set up the first national parks.

The history of environmentalism in most countries has followed a broadly similar pattern; an early period of pioneering and prophecy, culminating in recent decades in a widespread social movement. We might thus speak of a *first wave* of environmentalism, the initial response to the onset of industrialization, and a *second wave*, when a

largely intellectual response was given shape and force by a grounds-
well of public support. Environmentalism thus has a rather longer
and more distinguished lineage than is sometimes allowed for. In its
contemporary forms it is certainly a child of the nineteen sixties, but
also, as this book shows, perhaps a grandchild of the eighteen sixties.

The first wave of environmentalism proceeded step-by-step with
the Industrial Revolution, itself the most far-reaching process of social change in human history. The industrialization of the world dramatically altered the natural world through new methods of resource
extraction, production, and transportation. The scale and intensity
at which nature was used (and abused) increased manifold. Simultaneously, advances in medical technology led to a steady increase in
human populations. More humans producing more and consuming
more led axiomatically to greater pollution and habitat degradation.
The pace of environmental destruction greatly accelerated. Nature
became a source of cheap raw material as well as a sink for dumping
the unwanted residues of economic growth. Open-cast mining and
the ever-growing appetite of industry decimated forests and wild-
lands. New and dangerous chemicals were excreted into rivers and
the atmosphere.

The industrialization of Europe led also to major changes in the
rural economy. The factories and cities needed materials to process
and consume, these demands leading to a transformation of agriculture through the adoption of more capital-intensive, market-oriented
methods of production. Pastures and hedgerows and small farms with
mixed crops gave way to a more monotonous landscape, of large,
continuous holdings dominated by crop monocultures. Further afield,
European economic growth also impacted the natural environments
of Asia, Africa and North America. Industrialization had an organic
connection with imperial expansion, as white colonists took possession of large parts of the globe, re-orienting local economies towards
the demands of the metropolis. British ships were built of Burma
teak, their sailors wearing clothes of cotton grown in India, drinking
Kenyan coffee sweetened with sugar planted in the Caribbean. Decimating the forests of north-eastern United States, southern Africa
and the Western Ghats of India—to name only three such regions—
the British were, through the eighteenth and nineteenth centuries,
unquestionably the world leaders in deforestation. Emulating them
in lesser or greater degree were the Dutch, the Portuguese, the French,
the Belgians and the Germans, European powers who were to all become prime agents of ecological destruction in their colonies.

Environmental *problems* were certainly not unknown in the past, but possibly for the first time in human history there was now the perception of an environmental *crisis*. This was the perception seized upon by the first wave of environmentalism, which asked whether the great increases in wealth and prosperity brought about by modern industrialization were in fact sustainable. Notably, while the industrial city was the prime generator of ecological degradation, much of the burden of this degradation was felt in the country and the colony. As we shall see in this book, in the vanguard of the first wave of environmentalism were residents of the countryside, such as William Wordsworth, as well as unwilling subjects of colonialism, such as Mohandas Karamchand 'Mahatma' Gandhi.

As a dynamic social response to the Industrial Revolution, environmentalism bears comparison with three other movements of the modern world—democracy, socialism, and feminism. Defined in opposition to absolutism, democracy calls for a greater voice of ordinary citizens in decisions that affect their lives. Defined in opposition to both feudalism and capitalism, socialism calls for a more equitable distribution of wealth and productive resources. Defined in opposition to patriarchy, feminism calls for the granting of greater political and economic rights to women. Meanwhile the environmental movement has expanded human understandings of 'rights' and 'justice', calling for greater attention to the rights of nature as well as for sustainable lifestyles. Its agenda has sometimes been complementary to the agendas of other movements—at other times, in competition with them. These connections, between environmentalism on the one side and democracy, socialism or feminism on the other, shall be made explicit throughout this book.

Like all social movements, the environmental movement has within its fold different individuals, trends, traditions, and ideologies. Just as they are varieties of feminism, there have been varieties of environmentalism as well.

The first part of the book explores three such varieties, each a distinctive response to the emergence and impact of industrial society:

1. We have, first of all, the moral and cultural critique of the Industrial Revolution, here termed *back-to-the-land*. For the great romantic poets like Blake and Wordsworth, the 'dark, satanic mills' of the industrial age threatened to obliterate for ever their green and pleasant land, the pastoral idyll of rural and traditional England. Novelists like Charles Dickens and political thinkers like Friedrich Engels wrote critically of the inhuman working and living conditions of the time, the bleak

homes and the dark, damp and polluting factories. Others, like the Indian saint-politician Mahatma Gandhi, combined a moral critique with a simple lifestyle, living gently on the earth while deploring the multiplication of wants that modern civilization had brought about.

2. The second strand, that of *scientific conservation*, chose not to turn its back on industrial society, but to work instead on taming its excesses. Based on careful research in the empirical mode, rather than on a purely artistic or affective response, this variety of environmentalism argued that without careful guidance by experts industrialization would rapidly use up resources and pollute the environment. Conservation was the 'gospel of efficiency,' the use of science to manage nature and natural resources efficiently and in the long run. Crucial here is the idea of 'sustained yield,' the belief that human use of fish or forest, water or wildlife, should not dip into the capital stock, restricting itself to the annual increment of the resource in question. By the late nineteenth century, scientific conservation had emerged as a global movement, with foresters taking the lead in establishing resource management agencies run on scientific lines in Asia, Africa, Europe and North America.

3. The third strand of environmentalism, which combines elements of morality, science, and aesthetics, is what has come to be known as the *wilderness idea*. The industrialization of Europe, and the settlement and spread of European populations in the New World, devastated large areas of forest and wilderness. There arose in response a movement of artists and scientists which aimed to lock up areas still untouched, to keep them free of human disturbance. Sometimes the motivation was the protection from extinction of endangered species like the grizzly bear, at other times the saving of scenic habitats like Yosemite. Although it has its outposts in other corners too, the wilderness movement has flowered most vibrantly in the United States, as discussed in the pages of this book.

Back-to-the-land, *scientific conservation* and the *wilderness idea* constitute three generic modes of environmentalism. Part I of this book defines and documents these modes, tracing their evolution and expressions across the centuries and continents. In Part II we move forward to the second wave of environmentalism, its transformation from intellectual response to mass movement. Here we study the resurgence of the three distinctive strands in the 1960s and thereafter, and also explore the new dimensions brought to global environmentalism by the fears of a population explosion, the claims and assertions of women, and, especially, the divide between the rich countries of the North and the mostly poor countries of the South. We show how, in one country after another, there has arisen a vibrant and popular social movement dedicated to protecting or replenishing nature. Readers will note that while Part I starts with an examination of British traditions, Part II begins with an analysis of American trends. This choice is in keeping with our emphasis on industrialization as the generator of environmentalism. For the United Kingdom was the home of the original Industrial Revolution, while the United States has led the world in later elaborations of the industrial way of life. One country, consequently, pioneered the first wave of environmentalism; the other country showed the way in the second. Both parts of the book thereby uses an exemplary country as a springboard, to set off the subsequent discussion of environmentalism in other cultures. Our focus is as much on the differences as the similarities, for these 'national' movements have varied widely among themselves with regard to their tactics of protest and their ideas of what constitutes a worthwhile environment for us to nourish and live in.

III

To write a global history of anything, let alone a complex and widespread phenomenon such as environmentalism, is to be savagely selective. Inevitably, some of the more telling illustrations come from the histories of the two countries I am myself most familiar with, India and the United States. But I have tried to cast my net wider, to pick up examples and exemplars from times past and distant places. Where the Indian and American materials come from my own research, I have distilled from other peoples' writings and experiences the history of environmentalism in the countries of Asia and Latin America, as well as of Africa and Europe. Even so, some readers will complain that I have omitted their favourite country, others that I have not honored their favourite environmentalist.

There have been millions of words written on the history of American environmentalism, by historians and journalists, scientists and sociologists—all American. Following their lead, scholars elsewhere have written on the history of environmentalism in their own country. Studies of the United States still dominate the shelf of the library marked 'The Environmental Movement', but these are now being rapidly joined by works on the history of German, Swedish, British or Brazilian environmentalism. This book breaks with an established pattern, providing not another national history but a *trans*-national perspective on the environmental debate, by comparing and contrasting historical processes in six continents. By bringing in the experience of other cultures, and juxtaposing it with a fresh reading of environmentalism in the United States, the book hopes to set the American experience more properly in its global context.

A second aim of the book is to document the flow of ideas across cultures, the ways in which the environmental movement in one country has been transformed, invigorated and occasionally distorted by infusions from outside. Let me quickly run through some examples developed at length later. The founder of the United States Forest Service, Gifford Pinchot, honored as his mentor and prime inspiration a German botanist, Dietrich Brandis; it was Brandis who had previously set up the Forest Department in India, perhaps the largest and most influential of natural resource bureaucracies; this debt was returned with interest a century later when the ideas of Mahatma Gandhi were freely borrowed by the German Green Party, the most potent political expression of contemporary environmentalism. Gandhi himself is sometimes regarded as a quintessentially Indian, even Hindu thinker, yet he was deeply influenced by Russian populism (via the novelist, Leo Tolstoy, with whom he had been in correspondence); and by American radical individualism via Henry David Thoreau, whose essay on civil disobedience he regarded as his own political testament; and most significantly by English anti-industrialism via the works of the critic John Ruskin. Or take, finally, the movement of Deep Ecology, the leading edge of the American environmental movement today, which fights for 'biocentric equality,' that is, the placing of humans on par with and not above other species. While most of its adherents are to be found on the west coast of the United States, the ideas of Deep Ecology were first formulated by a Norwegian philosopher, Arné Naess, who once wrote a dissertation on—Gandhi!

The divides this book spans are, however, as much temporal as spatial. In the academy's division of labor, wherein historians study the past and sociologists and anthropologists study the present, earlier works have tended to concentrate on either the first or the second wave of environmentalism, rarely both. By contrast, this book locates the present in the past, showing the influence on contemporary movements of patterns and processes that have persisted over the years, or gone underground only to resurface once more. In this it draws inspiration from the Stanford poet, Wallace Stegner, who remarks that

> The tracing of ideas is a guessing game. We can't tell who first had an idea; we can only tell who first had it influentially, who formulated it in some form, poem or equation or picture, that others could stumble upon with the shock of recognition. The radical ideas that have been changing our attitudes towards our habitat have been around forever.

I would wish only to substitute, for the poet's 'forever', the less evocative but historically more precise phrase, 'at least for a hundred years'.

2

Back to the Land!

THE ENGLISH LOVE OF THE COUNTRY

In the eighteenth and nineteenth centuries the landscape of England was reshaped by the Industrial Revolution. Coal mines, textile mills, railroads and shipyards were the visible signs of an enormous expansion of industry and trade which made England the foremost economic power in the world. Industrialization was accompanied by rapid urbanization; between 1801 and 1911 the proportion of the British population living in cities increased from 20 per cent to 80 per cent. But the countryside was also being transformed, with a new breed of landowners producing wool, cotton and grain for the urban market. Peasants, shepherds and artisans, who had formed the backbone of the rural economy in medieval times, increasingly joined the ranks of the dispossessed, flocking to the cities in search of employment.

England was the home of industrialization, but also of opposition to it. The anthropologist Alan Macfarlane has captured this paradox well. In the mid-nineteenth century, he writes,

> England was the most urbanized country in the world, yet one where the yearning for the countryside and rural values was the most developed. Its strangely anti-urban bias was shown in the prevalence of parks, the ubiquity of flower gardens, the country holiday industry, the dreams of retirement to a honeysuckle cottage and the emphasis on 'nature' and rural values in the Romantic and pre-Raphaelite movements.

This affirmation of country life, in direct opposition to the emerging urban-industrial culture, was perhaps most eloquently expressed in a rich literary tradition, flowering in some of the finest works in the English language.

An early exemplar of this tradition was William Wordsworth (1770–1850), whose poetry expresses an intimate affinity with the natural world. During his lifetime Wordsworth walked some 175,000 miles through England, and, as the literary historian Jonathan Bate remarks, he taught his readers 'how to walk with nature' too. In his travels Wordsworth saw only 'the darker side of the great change' wrought by the Industrial Revolution: the 'outrage done to nature' by the cities and factories, such that the common people were no longer 'breathing fresh air' or 'treading the green earth.' The poet was profoundly out of sympathy with the morés of city life, with its impersonality and its elevation of money-making above all other values. In the country, and only there, lay 'the secret spirit of humanity,' which, despite war, revolution and economic change,

> 'mid the calm oblivious tendencies
> of nature, 'mid her plants, her weeds and flowers,
> And silent overgrowings, still survived.

Underlying Wordsworth's poetry and philosophy was a defense of the organic union with nature of the peasant and shepherd, a way of life that the deadly combination of industrialization and market farming wished to obliterate. Although village folk were illiterate and inarticulate, they were in closer touch with nature than the city dweller. 'And grossly that man errs,' he wrote, 'who should suppose'—

> That the green Valleys, and the Streams and Rocks
> Were things indifferent to the Shepherd's thoughts.
> Fields, where with cheerful spirits he had breath'd
> The common air; the hills which he so oft
> Had climb'd with vigorous steps; which had impress'd
> So many incidents upon his mind
> Of hardship, skill or courage, joy or fear;
> Which like a book preserv'd the memory
> Of the dumb animals, whom he had sav'd,
> Had fed or shelter'd . . .
>   these fields, these hills
> Which were his living Being, even more
> Than his own Blood—what could they less? had laid
> Strong hold on his affections, were to him
> A pleasurable feeling of blind love,
> The pleasure which is there in life itself.

This is from a poem about the shepherds of the Lake District, the region with which Wordsworth is most closely identified. He even wrote a guide to the people and scenery of the Lakes: a book now forgotten, but a bestseller in its day, which earned him more money than his most celebrated poems. Indeed, in the last years of his life Wordsworth was moved to begin a public campaign against the extension of the railway to the Lake District, a development he feared would disrupt the beauty and integrity of the region.

Wordsworth's book on his favorite place was published in various editions, under various titles. The 1842 version had an expansive title, redolent of the nineteenth century: it was published as *A Complete Guide to the Lakes, Comprising Minute Directions for the Tourist, with Mr Wordsworth's Description of the Scenery of the Country, etc. And Three Letters on the Geology of the Lake District, by the Rev. Professor Sedgwick, Edited by the Publisher*. By any name it was rather more than a brochure, and little less than a summation of the poet's natural credo. In his book *Romantic Ecology*, Jonathan Bate nicely places Wordsworth in the context of his own time and ours. The values of the Guide, he says, were

> the maintaining of the place for the benefit of the whole nation; the conception of landscape beauty, with a particular emphasis on wild (sublime) country; the belief in the importance of the open air; the respect for buildings that have a history in the place; and the recognition that traditional agricultural practices are integral to the identity of the place. Wordsworth would have been pleased that shepherds still work on the hills of Westmorland and Cumberland, since, in contrast to the American model, the English and Welsh National Parks do not consist of enclosed areas owned by the government; the land in them remains privately owned . . . Conservation is sought by means of planning rather than possession.

One of Wordsworth's junior contemporaries was John Clare (1793–1864), a poet from farming stock. Clare's best-known verses deal with the impact of the enclosure, by rich landowners, of village common land to raise crops for the urban market. Enclosure threw the rural poor out of work and destroyed the diversity of life-forms that had long been a feature of the English landscape. Clare's poem *The Village Ministrel* speaks of how—

> There once were lanes in nature's freedom dropt,
> There once were paths that every valley wound—
> Inclosure came, and every path was stopt;
> Each tyrant fix'd his sign where paths were found,
> To hint a tresspass now who cross'd the ground:

Justice is made to speak as they command;
The high road must now be each stinted bound:
—Inclosure, thou'rt a curse upon the land,
And tasteless was the wretch who thy existence plann'd . . .
. . . Ye fields, ye scenes so dear to Lubin's eye,
Ye meadow-blooms, ye pasture-flowers, farewell!
Ye banish'd trees, ye make me deeply sigh,
Inclosure came, and all your glories fell.

Next in the English tradition of romantic environmentalists lies John Ruskin (1819–1900), artist, art critic, sometime Professor of Poetry at the University of Oxford. Ruskin thought modern towns 'little more than laboratories for the distillation into heaven of venomous smokes and smells, mixed with effluvia from decaying animal matter, and infectious miasmata from purulent disease.' The air was foul, and the water too, for every river in England had been turned 'into a common sewer, so that you cannot so much as baptize an English baby but with filth, unless you hold its face out in the rain, and even that falls dirty.' This destruction, he thought, owed itself to the fact that modern man had *desacralized* nature, viewing it only as a source of raw materials to be exploited, and thus emptying it of the mystery, the wonder, indeed the divinity with which pre-modern man saw the natural world. Observe the contrast at work through Ruskin's luminous prose:

> Whereas the mediaeval never painted a cloud, but with the purpose of placing an angel in it; and a Greek never entered a wood without expecting to meet a god in it; we should think the appearance of an angel in the cloud wholly unnatural, and should be seriously surprised by meeting a god anywhere. Our chief ideas about the wood are connected with poaching. We have no belief that the clouds contain more than so many inches of rain or hail, and from our ponds and ditches expect nothing more divine than ducks and watercresses.

Unlike Wordsworth, Ruskin focused closely on the physical consequences of the industrialization of England: the befouling of the air and of the waters, as well as the impact of this pollution on human health and the landscape. But the influence of the poet on his work is manifest, never more so when, in 1876, he launched a fresh campaign (see *box*) to prevent the extension of the railroad into the Lake District. Ruskin believed that the trains, and the hordes of tourists they might bring, would destroy the District. As with Wordsworth, Ruskin's love of the land was inseparable from his love of the rustic who dwelled in it. In opposing the railways he wished as much to protect

RUSKIN OPPOSES THE RAILWAYS, DEFENDS THE LAKES

In John Ruskin the passion of the environmentalist fused with the eloquence of a great prose stylist.

When the frenzy of avarice is daily drowning our sailors, suffocating our miners, poisoning our children, and blasting the cultivable surface of England into a treeless waste of ashes, what does it really matter whether a flock of sheep, more or less, be driven from the slopes of Helvellyn, or the little pool of Thirlmere filled with shale, or a few wild blossoms of St. John's vale lost to the coronal of English spring? Little to any one; and—let me say this, at least, in the outset of all saying—*nothing to me.* No one need charge me with selfishness in any word or action for defence of these mossy hills. I do not move, with such small activity as I have yet shown in the business, because I live at Coniston (where no sound of the iron wheels by Dunmail Raise can reach me), nor because I can find no other place to remember Wordsworth by than the daffodil margin of his little Rydal marsh. What thoughts and work are yet before me, such as he taught, must be independent of any narrow associations. All my own dear mountain grounds and treasure-cities, Chamouni, Interlachen, Lucerne, Geneva, Venice, are long ago destroyed by the European populace; and now, for my own part, I don't care what more they do; they may drain Loch Katrine, drink Loch Lomond, and blow all Wales and Cumberland into a heap of slate shingle; the world is wide enough yet to find me some refuge during the days appointed for me to stay in. But it is no less my duty, in the cause of those to whom the sweet landscapes of England are yet precious, and to whom they may yet teach what they taught me, in early boyhood, and would still if I had not to learn,—it is my duty to plead with what earnestness I may, that these sacred sibylline books may be redeemed from perishing.

. . . I have said I take no selfish interest in this resistance to the railroad. But I do take an unselfish one. It is precisely because I passionately wish to improve the minds of the populace, and because I am spending my own mind, strength, and fortune, wholly on that object, that I don't want to let them see Hellvellyn while they are drunk. I suppose few men now living have so earnestly felt—none certainly have so earnestly declared— that the beauty of nature is the blessedest and most necessary of lessons for men; and that all other efforts in education are futile till you have taught your people to love fields, birds, and flowers. Come then, my benevolent friends, join with me in that teaching.

Source: 'The Extension of Railways in the Lake District' (1876), in *The Works of John Ruskin, Volume XXXIV*, edited by E. T. Cook and Alexander Wedderburn (London: George Allen, 1908), pp. 137–8, 142.

nature as the moral fibre of the villagers 'whose strength and virtue yet survive to represent the body and soul of England before her days of mechanical decrepitude and commercial dishonour.'

His writings apart, Ruskin also worked to build institutions which would recapture the flavor of a world rapidly being lost. He set up a guild, named for St. George, that ran farms and craft shops which stressed self-sufficiency and simplicity, producing food and weaving cloth for their own use. The revival of handicrafts was also vigorosly promoted by his disciple William Morris (1834–96), likewise a man mostly out of step with his times, a man who—as the writer Jan Marsh points out—'wished as far as possible to live in the fourteenth rather than the nineteenth century.'

Poet, prophet, designer, architect and socialist, William Morris lived a life of many parts; he has since been claimed as an ancestor by numerous artistic and political movements. But the environmental movement has as good a claim as any. A native Londoner, Morris deplored the city's growth, its 'swallowing up with its loathsomeness field and wood and heath without mercy and without hope, mocking our feeble attempts to deal even with its minor evils of smoke-laden sky and befouled river.' Morris wished to turn England 'from the grimy backyard of a workshop into a garden,' from which factories would disappear, with town and country resuming a relation of harmony and mutual benefit. His long narrative poem 'The Earthly Paradise' begins by asking the reader to—

Forget six counties overhung with smoke,
Forget the snorting steam and piston stroke,
Forget the spreading of the hideous town;
Think rather of the pack-horse on the down,
And dream of London, small, and white, and clean,
The clear Thames bordered by its gardens green . . .

We move on, finally, to Edward Carpenter (1844–1929), an associate of Morris with whom the English back-to-the-land movement finally turned international. Trained as a mathematician, ordained as a priest, Carpenter resigned holy orders and a prestigious Cambridge fellowship to move back to the land. With some friends he set up a commune on a hill above the factory town of Sheffield, offering a union of manual labor and clean air as an alternative to industrial civilization. In this he was influenced by Morris, but also by the Americans Walt Whitman and Henry David Thoreau, whose message of the simple life he enthusiastically embraced. The commune grew its own food and vegetables and baked its own bread; its members, who included men from working class backgrounds, discarded most of their clothing as superfluous. Their farm has been described as 'a true Arcadia; three fields running down to a brook, a wooded valley below and the moors above.' The contrast with Sheffield could be sharply etched, and looking down on the town in May 1889, Carpenter saw—

> only a vast dense cloud, so thick that I wondered how any human being could support life in it, that went up to heaven like the smoke from a great altar. An altar, indeed, it seemed to me, wherein thousands of lives were being yearly sacrificed. Beside me on the hills the sun was shining, the larks were singing; but down there a hundred thousand grown people, let alone children, were struggling for a little sun and air, toiling, moiling, living a life of suffocation, dying (as the sanitary reports only too clearly show) of diseases caused by foul air and want of light—all for what? To make a few people rich!

The writings of Wordsworth, Ruskin, Morris and Carpenter helped inspire the establishment of an array of environmental societies in the late nineteenth century. These included the Commons Preservation Society, begun in 1865 to prevent the encroachment of cities on woodland and heath used by communities for recreation; the Society for the Protection of Ancient Buildings, founded by William Morris himself in 1877; the Lake District Defence Society, stoutly in the Wordsworth–Ruskin lineage, which was formed in 1883; the Selborne League, created in 1885 for the protection of rare birds, beautiful plants, and threatened landscapes, and named for the great eighteenth-century naturalist Gilbert White of Selbourne; and the Coal Smoke Abatement Society, influenced by Edward Carpenter's writings, and started in 1898 as an independent pressure group to make the government enforce pollution control laws on errant factories. Preceding all of these was the Scottish Rights of Way Society, formed in 1843 to protect walking areas around the city of Edinburgh.

One of the most influential of these societies has been the National Trust, which was created in 1895. A prime mover behind the setting up of the Trust was Octavia Hill (1838–1912), quite possibly the first woman environmentalist of significance. A friend of Ruskin, Hill, like her compatriots, coupled environmental protection with social reform and was a pioneer in establishing clean and congenial dwellings for the urban poor. She was active in many environmental campaigns: she organized the first anti-smoke exhibition in London and, as a member of the Commons Preservation Society, helped protect numerous areas of the city from encroachment or deterioration. As the *Dictionary of National Biography* notes, 'it was largely due to her efforts that Parliament Hill and many other large and small open spaces were secured for public use and enjoyment.' Octavia Hill also helped define the objectives of the National Trust, which were outlined in its first annual report:

> to promote the permanent preservation, for the benefit of the Nation, of land and tenements (including buildings) of beauty or historic interest; and as regards lands, to preserve (so far as practicable) their natural aspects, features, and animal and plant life; and for this purpose to accept from private owners of property, gifts and places of interest or beauty, and to hold the lands, houses and other property thus acquired, in trust for the use and enjoyment of the nation.

These aims are much broader than the protection of old buildings and stately homes, the activities for which the National Trust is now chiefly known. At the same time, they were much narrower than the aims of John Ruskin or Edward Carpenter, which were to turn the clock back, to restore England as a country of cozy villages and manageable small towns nestling within a landscape of pretty pastures, luxuriant oak forests, and clean swift-flowing rivers. Indeed, throughout history visionary aims have served as the source of more modest or, one might say, *piecemeal* reform. By setting aside forests and wetlands, or preserving historic buildings and parks, the environmental societies begun in the late nineteenth century have saved at least some parts of England from the contaminating effects of urban-industrial civilization. This represents the tangible fruits of the back-to-the-land movement, the putting into practice, albeit in a limited way, of the ideas and aspirations of Ruskin and company. The international influence of these English visionaries will be explored later in the chapter. But we must first take a small detour.

A DETOUR: WERE THE NAZIS GREEN, AND ARE GREENS NAZIS?

By the late nineteenth century, Germany had surpassed England as the front-runner in technological and industrial development. Here too, poets and writers were in the vanguard of the movement to keep their land rural and their forests virgin, uncontaminated by the greed of the cities and the excrement of their factories. Consider these lines from a poem published in 1901 by Rainer Maria Rilke:

> Everything will again be great and mighty,
> The land simple and the water bountiful,
> The trees gigantic and the walls very small.
> And in the valleys strong and multiformed,
> A nation of shepherds and peasant farmers.

A nation of peasants and shepherds, not of factory workers and entre-
peneurs, which was in fact what Germany was fast becoming. In the
Rilkean vision peasants were celebrated as the backbone of the nation, but the forests were more important still, as the repository of
German culture, the inspiration for its poets, musicians, and artists.
The self-proclaimed sociologist 'of field and forest,' William Heinrich
Reill, wrote in 1861 that the woods 'were the heartland of [German]
folk culture . . . so that a village without a forest is like a town without any historical buildings, theater or art galleries. Forests are games
fields for the young, feasting-places for the old.' But by making the
peasant into a market-driven farmer, and by destroying forests or
converting then into timber plantations, industrialization was un-
dermining the very basis of 'German-ness.' In the German romantic
tradition environmentalism was united with patriotism, such that
peasants, forests and the nation came to constitute an organic whole.
'The German people need the forest like man needs wine,' wrote a
nineteenth-century theologian, adding: 'We must preserve the forest, not simply so that the oven does not grow cold in winter but also
in order that the pulse of the national life continues to beat warm
and happy [in order that] Germany remains German.'

Of course, in England as much as in Germany, rural romantics
were in a distinct minority. The dominant industrial culture of the
two countries met in the First World War, a conflict which first revealed the awesome destructive power of modern technology. To some
observers the costs of war—some ten million dead—were the consequence wholly of industrialization and capitalist development,
through the hunger for territory and the forces of avarice that they
had unleashed. Indeed no sooner had the conflict ended that there
occurred a revival of the agrarian ideal throughout Europe. This took
various forms: the establishment of a Council for the Protection of
Rural England in 1928; the growth of agrarian parties in Eastern
Europe to defend the peasant from exploitation by the city dweller;
and the spread of ruralist ideas in Scandinavia through the work of
the novelist Knut Hamsun, who spent his Nobel Prize money on restoring an old farm.

In Germany the reassertion of peasant environmentalism in the
1920s was accompanied by the rise of the National Socialists. There
was unquestionably, at times, a congruence between the views of environmentalists and Nazis. Some Nazi thinkers also emphasized a
mystic unity between the peasant, the forest, and the national spirit.
Others railed against the growth of the cities. The party's newspaper worried in 1932 that 'the influence of the metropolis has grown

overwhelmingly strong. Its asphalt culture is destroying peasant think-ing, the rural lifestyle, and [national] strength.' Leading Nazis were prominent in environmental causes. The Minister for Agriculture, Walter Darré, was an enthusiast for organic farming. Herman Göering, second only to Adolf Hitler in the party hierarchy, strongly sup-ported nature protection, appointing himself Master of the German Hunt as well as Master of the German Forests.

The apparent affinity between Nazism and green ideology has led some commentators to claim that environmentalism is conduc-ive to authoritarian thinking. When the German Green Party was formed in the 1970s (a development explored in Chapter Five), some of its opponents darkly suggested that the National Socialists were the first 'Green party.' The historian Raymond Dominick, after a careful study of the subject, points out, however, that 'although sev-eral substantial areas of agreement drew National Socialism together, to cross over into the Nazi camp a conservationist had to accept blat-ant racism.' In the Nazi slogan of 'Blut und Boden' (Blood and Soil) many environmentalists identified only with the latter part. More-over, in practice the Nazis built an industrial economy—in part to ready themselves for war—that was totally at odds with the peasant ideology they sometimes claimed to uphold. The journalist Sebastian Haffner, who was forced into exile by Hitler's regime, wrote in 1944 that as 'soon as the Nazis took over in Germany they began fever-ishly to build. First came technical construction work, motor roads, aerodromes, armanent factories, fortifications:' scarcely the agenda of environmentalists. As one of their leading architects, with a sheaf of commissions in hand, put it, the Nazis wished to give 'permanent evidence in concrete and marble of the greatness of our time.' They also vigorously promoted consumerism; Hitler once promised every German citizen a Volkswagen car and built in anticipation highways to drive them on. In the wry judgement of the Spanish scholar Juan Martinez Alier, the reality of Nazi rule was not *Blut und Boden* but rather *Blut und Autobahnen*.

Some Nazis were indeed Green, but most were not. In any event, to be Green—then or now—is not connected with being Nazi.

THE GANDHIAN VIEW OF THE SIMPLE LIFE

In 1889 Edward Carpenter published *Civilization: Its Cause and Cure*, a book which has been termed a 'kind of text for the back-to-the-land movement.' One of its early and admiring readers was a twenty-year-old Indian who had recently arrived to study law in London.

The Indian did not know Carpenter, but soon became intimate with his disciple Henry Salt, a pacifist and animal rights activist who likewise preached a return to nature and praised the simplicity of rural life. It was in Salt's *Journal of the Vegetarian Society* that the young man published his first writings, the beginnings of an oeuvre that came to comprise ninety closely printed volumes.

The Indian was Mohandas Karamchand Gandhi, a political and spiritual leader of consummate skill and considerable achievement, regarded by the *International Herald Tribune*, and by countless other organizations and individuals, as the greatest person of the twentieth century. Mahatma Gandhi is celebrated as a doughty opponent of racism in South Africa, where he lived, and struggled, for over twenty years; as an Indian freedom fighter whose opposition to British rule helped inspire numerous anti-colonial movements in Asia and Africa; and as the perfector of a technique of non-violent protest that has since been used in a variety of contexts, from the civil rights movement in the United States to Solidarity in Poland. All this notwithstanding, he was also an early environmentalist who anticipated the damaging effects on nature of the industrial economy and the consumer society.

In his autobiography, Gandhi recalled that of the books he read in his youth, 'the one which brought about an instantaneous and practical transformation in my life was [John Ruskin's] *Unto This Last*.' John Ruskin and Edward Carpenter are both acknowledged in Gandhi's first book, *Hind Swaraj* (Indian Home Rule), published in 1909. In this work Gandhi decisively rejects industrialization as an option for India, then a colony struggling to free itself from British rule. For industrial society, as Gandhi had observed it in the West—in person and through the writings of Ruskin and company—was selfish, competitive, and grossly destructive of nature. He thought that 'the distinguishing characteristic of modern civilization is an indefinite multiplication of wants,' to satisfy which one had to forage far and wide for raw materials and commodities. Gandhi believed that by contrast preindustrial civilizations were marked by an 'imperative restriction upon, and a strict regulating of, these wants.' In uncharacteristically intemperate tones, he spoke of 'wholeheartedly detest[ing] this mad desire to destroy distance and time, to increase animal appetites, and go to the ends of the earth in search of their satisfaction. If modern civilization stands for all this, and I have understood it to do so, I call it satanic.'

Gandhi offered, as an alternative, a code of voluntary simplicity that minimized wants and recycled resources—his own letters were

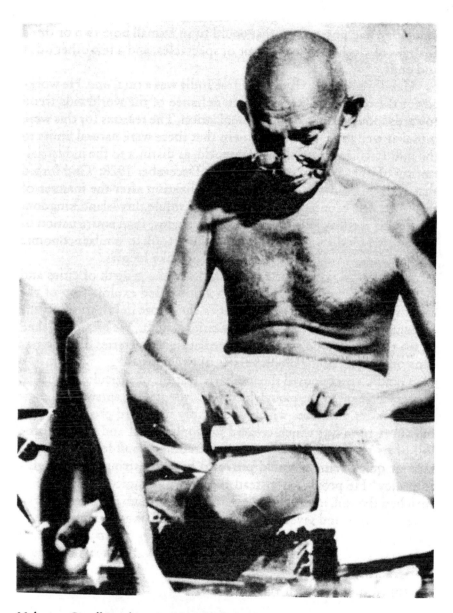

Mahatma Gandhi, at his spinning wheel, circa *1946.*
SOURCE Unidentified Photographer.

written on the back of used paper. One of Gandhi's best known aphorisms is: 'The world has enough for everybody's need, but not enough for one person's greed:' an exquisitely phrased one-line environmental ethic. It was an ethic he himself practised; when he died in January 1948 this man, whose followers were reckoned in the tens of millions, and who helped bring down one of the most powerful empires in history, had possessions that could fit in a small box: two or three changes of clothes, a clock, a pair of spectacles, and a few other odds and ends.

Gandhi's broader vision for a free India was a rural one. He worked for the renewal of its villages, in defiance of the worldwide trend towards industrialization and urbanization. The reasons for this were moral as well as ecological—namely, that there were natural limits to the industrialization of the whole world, as distinct to the industrialization of one country. As he wrote in December 1928: 'God forbid that India should ever take to industrialization after the manner of the West. The economic imperialism of a single tiny island kingdom [England] is today keeping the world in chains. If an entire nation of 300 million [India's population at the time] took to similar economic exploitation, it would strip the world bare like locusts.'

For Gandhi, as for Ruskin and Morris, the growth of cities and factories was possible only through a one-sided exploitation of the countryside. 'The blood of the villages,' he wrote in July 1946, 'is the cement with which the edifice of the cities is built.' He himself wished to see that 'the blood that is today inflating the arteries of the cities runs once again in the blood vessels of the villages.'

Gandhi also opposed the industrialization of agriculture, that is, the replacement of the plough by the tractor and the spread of chemical fertilizers, measures which undeniably increased productivity in the short term but which created unemployment and depleted the soil of its nutrients. He warned that 'trading in soil fertility for the sake of quick returns would prove to be a disastrous, short-sighted policy.' He promoted instead the use of organic manure, which enriched the soil, improved village hygiene through the effective disposal of waste, and saved valuable foreign exchange. But the revitalization of the rural economy also depended on the revival of craft industry (see *box* for his vision of village renewal). India's once vibrant traditions of weaving and other handicrafts had been largely destroyed under British rule, and to restore them Gandhi created two organizations: an All India Village Industries Association and an All India Spinners' Association.

These organizations were run by one of Gandhi's close followers, J. C. Kumarappa, an economist to whom he entrusted the work of village reconstruction. Kumarappa had studied accountancy in London and economics at Columbia University in New York, before joining the Indian nationalist movement in the 1920s. Working with Gandhi, Kumarappa explored the relation between peasant agriculture and the natural world. For Indian peasants the cultivation of the soil was made possible only by the flow of nutrients from outside: water from ponds and rivers, and manure from cattle dung and from the forest. This meant that the careful management of common property resources, such as irrigation tanks and grazing grounds, was as important to agricultural production as the management of privately owned plots of farmland. There had once existed vigorous village-level institutions for this purpose, which had decayed under British rule. Water and pasture were gifts of nature that were central to peasant farming in India: and in Kumarappa's view, the revival of collective institutions for their management was an important task for economic policy in free India.

AN IDEAL VILLAGE

Gandhi's prosaic, down-to-earth description of his ideal Indian village, offered in January 1937.

It will have cottages with sufficient light and ventilation, built of a material obtainable within a radius of five miles of it. The cottages will have courtyards enabling householders to plant vegetables for domestic use and to house their cattle. The village lanes and streets will be free of all avoidable dust. It will have wells according to its needs and accessible to all. It will have houses of worship for all, also a common meeting place, a village common for grazing its cattle, a co-operative dairy, primary and secondary schools in which industrial [i.e. vocational] education will be the central fact, and it will have Panchayats [village councils] for settling disputes. It will produce its own grains, vegetables and fruit, and its own Khadi [hand-spun cotton]. This is roughly my idea of a model village . . .

Source: *Collected Works of Mahatma Gandhi*, Volume *LXIV* (New Delhi: Publications Division, 1976), p. 217.

Like his master, Kumarappa believed that an 'economy of permanence' could be founded only on agriculture. 'There can be no industrialization without predation,' he observed, whereas agriculture is, and ought to be, 'the greatest among occupations,' in which 'man attempts to control nature and his own environment in such a way as to produce the best results.' This contrast could be expressed in terms of their relative impact on the natural world. Thus—

in the case of an agricultural civilization, the system ordained by nature is not interfered with to any great extent. If there is a variation at all, it follows a natural mutation. The agriculturist only aids nature or intensifies in a short time what takes place in nature in a long period . . . Under the economic system of [industrial society] . . . we find that variations from nature are very violent in that a large supply of goods is produced irrespective of demand, and then a demand is artificially created for goods by means of clever advertisements.

Comparing the philosophies of Ruskin and Gandhi, the eminent Indian economist M. L. Dantwala has remarked that for both thinkers 'industrialization was the culprit which destroyed their idyll of a peaceful self-sufficient rural society, in which workers bought their own raw materials, spun and wove them and sold their finished goods to the rural community.' The Gandhian version of the simple life did indeed follow the English model in several respects: in its focus on manual labor, in its elevation of the village as the supreme form of human society, in its corresponding rejection of industrial culture as violent, competitive and destructive of nature and thus unsustainable in the long run. To quote Dantwala once more, the work of Gandhi and Ruskin is best understood as 'a reaction to the egregious excesses of adolescent industrialization.' Nonetheless, the Indian tradition is to be distinguished from the English in at least two respects. First, the Gandhian vision was a severely practical one, ridding itself of the lyric romanticism of Wordsworth and company. Gandhi had little time for art or poetry or music; his concerns were resolutely focused on the economic and the political, the restoring of the livelihoods and dignity of villagers subjugated by the cities and by British colonial rule. Second, in the England of the nineteenth century peasants and craftsmen had been more or less extinguished by the Industrial Revolution; going back-to-the-land was in this sense an act of defiance, quite out of step with the dominant ethos. It might, through pressure groups and environmental societies, moderate the progress of industrialization, but it could scarcely hope to halt it. By contrast, while Gandhi and Kumarappa worked and wrote India was a land of 700,000 villages whose traditional methods of farming, pastoralism and craft production still had a fair chance of withstanding competition from factory-made products. The agrarian ideal for Ruskin was just that—an ideal; whereas for Gandhi it might just conceivably have formed the basis for social renewal in a free India.

3

The Ideology of Scientific Conservation

CONSERVATION INTERNATIONALISM

In May 1864 the well-known New York firm of Charles Scribners published a volume called *Man and Nature: Or, Physical Geography as Modified by Human Action*. The book was based on years of careful study and reflection, but the author, a Vermont scholar and diplomat named George Perkins Marsh, expected it to have little impact. So doubtful was Marsh of the book's sales that he donated the copyright to the United States Sanitary Commission. Thoughtful friends purchased the copyright and gave it back to the author; a prudent move, for, contrary to Marsh's expectations, *Man and Nature* was to achieve canonical status as the book that sparked the first wave of American environmentalism. As the historian and critic Lewis Mumford once remarked, Marsh's opus was the 'fountainhead of the conservation movement,' a 'comprehensive ecological study before the very word ecology had been invented.'

In the same year as Marsh's book first appeared, a German botanist employed by the government of British India was invited to head a newly created, countrywide, Forest Service. This man, Dietrich Brandis, knew and corresponded with Marsh; he shared with the American a concern with the pace of deforestation and an abiding faith in the powers of scientific expertise to reverse it. The Indian Forest

Department, which Brandis headed for close on two decades, has been one of the most influential institutions in the history of conservation. Established in 1864, by the turn of the century it came to control a little over a fifth of India's land area. It was by far the biggest landlord in a very large country, a status it continues to enjoy to this day.

Although separated by some 10,000 miles, the American publication of *Man and Nature* and the formation of the Indian Forest Department should be viewed as part of the same historical process. From the late eighteenth century, Western scientists had begun exploring the links between deforestation, desiccation, and drought. The rapid clearance of forests, due to agricultural colonization and industrial development, contributed to accelerated soil erosion, and even, some scientists argued, to a decline in rainfall. In North America as well as in the Continent, the growth of human populations and the expansion of trade and industry led to a crisis in the availability of wood products and a steep rise in their price. In Africa and Asia too, the dynamic forces unleashed by European colonialism led to massive environmental degradation, as rainforests in the hills were converted to tea plantations and pastures in the plains replaced by commercial crops such as cotton and sugarcane.

A pioneering analyst of global deforestation was the German scientist and explorer Alexander von Humboldt (1769–1859). From a study of the fluctuating levels of a Venezuelan lake he drew these general conclusions:

> The changes which the destruction of forests, the clearing of plants and the cultivation of indigo have produced within half a century in the quantity of water flowing in on the one hand, and on the other the evaporation of the soil and the dryness of the atmosphere, present causes sufficiently powerful to explain the successive diminution of the lake of Valencia . . . By felling the trees that cover the tops and sides of mountains, men in every climate prepare at once two calamities for future generations, the want of fuel and the scarcity of water. . . . When forests are destroyed, as they are everywhere in America by the European planters, with an improvident precipitation, the springs are entirely dried up, or become less abundant. The beds of rivers, remaining dry during a part of the year, are converted into torrents, whenever great rain falls on the heights. The sward and the moss disappearing with the brushwoods from the sides of the mountains, the waters falling in rain are no longer impeded in their course, and instead of slowly augmenting the level of the rivers by progressive filtrations, they furrow during heavy showers the sides of the hills, beat down the loosened soil and

form these sudden inundations that devastate the country. Hence it results that the destruction of forests, the want of permanent springs and the existence of torrents are three phenomena closely connected together. Countries that are situated in opposite hemispheres, Lombardy bordered by the chain of the Alps and Lower Peru inclosed between the Pacific Ocean and the Cordillera of the Andes, exhibit striking proofs of the justness of this assertion.

The British historian Richard Grove correctly observes that these observations of 1819 'have not been superseded by more recent findings'. But Humboldt was, as Grove further reminds us, but the most sophisticated among a group of like-minded conservationists. In both metropolis and colony, the process of habitat destruction was viewed with horror by these conservation-minded scientists. Where private greed—notably, the pioneer's plow and the lumberman's axe—had contributed to deforestation, scientists believed that prompt intervention in the form of public ownership of forests and other natural resources might arrest environmental decline and provide a basis for steady economic growth. Crucial here was the idea of *sustained yield*, based on the belief that scientists could accurately estimate the annual increment of renewable natural resources like wood and water, fish and wildlife. Scientists prescribed that utilization stayed within this increment, thus maintaining nature's capital and ensuring a yield capable of being 'sustained' in the long term.

George Perkins Marsh in North America, and Dietrich Brandis in South Asia, were in the vanguard of what was to emerge as a scientific movement of truly global consequence. By the middle of the nineteenth century, the centralization of political authority and the formation of nation-states allowed experts to intervene more broadly, on a national scale, in the planning and management of natural resources. It began to make sense to speak of 'national forests,' or of 'rivers as the property of the nation,' where previously these resources were recognized largely as being locally owned and controlled, by villages, tribes, or municipalities. The growing prestige of science, and its ever closer alliance with the state, helped foresters and irrigation engineers, soil conservationists as well as wildlife managers, build numerous institutions based on sustained-yield principles in different parts of the world. Some of the more extensive and powerful of these institutions were to be found in the European colonies of Asia and Africa, where authoritarian state systems allowed for the exercise of scientific conservation unconstrained by parliaments, a free press, or the practice of democracy more generally.

To locate scientific conservation in its international context, let us consider the following developments, all of which occurred ten years either side of the publication of G. P. Marsh's *Man and Nature*. In 1859, a Forest and Herbiage Protection Act was passed by the Government of the Cape Colony of Southern Africa, allowing the state to intervene and take over areas of veld and forest threatened with destruction. The next year, 1860, the governor-general of colonial Java formed a committee to plan forest legislation for the island, the epicenter of the Netherlands' overseas empire. Laws protecting Java's forests and affirming state control over them were passed in 1865, also the year of the first Indian Forest Act. Already in 1862, the French had promulgated the first of a series of ordinances designed to create forest reserves in their colonies in Cochinchina (present-day Vietnam). Further east, the 1870s witnessed a flurry of forest-related activities in the British colony of Australia. Thus the province of Victoria appointed a Royal Forestry Commission in 1871, while South Australia passed a Forest Tree Act two years later. Australian forest enthusiasts frequently used Marsh's findings as supporting evidence (see *box*); meanwhile, at the other end of the world, *Man and Nature* was acquiring belated attention at home. The book stimulated the American Association for the Advancement of Science to submit a petition to Congress in 1873, urging the establishment of a national forestry system and the creation of forest reserves.

As these examples illustrate, foresters were unquestionably in the lead of a scientific movement that also counted, among its constituents, votaries of sustained-yield soil, water, wildlife and fisheries management. This movement was held together by a set of beliefs that was remarkably invariant across the continents and across the different sectors in which it was applied. In the phrase of the South African scholar William Beinart, scientific conservation was an ideology of 'doom and resurrection,' predicting that agricultural and industrial expansion would destroy the environment unless replaced, forthwith, by more rational and far-seeing forms of resource use. Here the conservationist singled out the pioneer farmer for special attention, or, should one say, special condemnation. Thus, one colonial soil scientist remarked in 1908 on the tendency of European settlers in African colonies to 'scoop out the richest and most beautiful valleys, leaving them dry and barren.' Or, as a Scottish forester working in the same continent put it: 'Is it not the case that the history of civilized man in his colonisation of new countries has been in every age substantially this—he has found the country a wilderness; he has cut down trees, and he has left it a desert.' Again, the head of the

United States Soil Conservation Service wrote in 1935 that 'the ultimate consequence of unchecked soil erosion when it sweeps over whole countries as it is doing today must be national extinction.'

SCIENTIFIC CONSERVATION
IN AUSTRALIA

A year after the publication of George Perkins Marsh's Man and Nature, *a Melbourne newspaper reprised the book's message for its own readers. Note the global reach of the discussion, the cautionary tales as well as the positive lessons gleaned from the experience of other lands.*

Over and over again we have urged that steps should be taken to protect our forest lands, not only because extravagance will lead to scarcity, but also because the local climate will be affected in all those places where the forests are removed. In protecting the forests we do more than increase the growth of timber—we prevent waste of soil, we conserve the natural streams, it is not improbable that we prevent decrease in the rainfall, and it is certain that we largely affect the distribution of storm waters. A covering of shrubs and grasses protects the loose soil from being carried away by floods . . . The Italian hydrographers have made mention very often of the disastrous results attendant on destruction of forests—Frisi relates that when the natural woods were removed from the declivities of the Upper Val d'Arno, in Tuscany, the soil of the hills was washed down to the Arno in vast quantities, to the great injury of the riparian proprietors. Some districts of Catalonia have suffered even more by the incautious operations of man; and, on the other hand, we know by what has been done in Italy, in France, in Germany and in Algeria, how much the local climate may be ameliorated, and the fruitfulness of gardens and fields increased by judicious planting.

. . . The reservation of large tracts of forests is our first duty. By keeping the hills clothed we may make fruitful the valleys, and provide stores of moisture for the parched plains. . . . Carefully managed, we have much wealth in our forests. The miner, the agriculturalist, and the housebuilder, notwithstanding that their demands are large, can be fully supplied if extravagance be checked and waste be prevented. As the old trees are removed others should be planted. We may with advantage take a lesson from Mehemet Ali and Ibrahim Pacha, who planted more than 20 million of trees in Egypt . . . The conservation of the forest lands, and the extension and improvement of them, concern alike the landholder and the miner, and should occupy the attention of everyone who has leisure and means to become a co-worker with nature.

Source: *The Argus*, Melbourne, 16 October 1865, quoted in
J. M. Powell, *Environmental Management in Australia, 1788–1914*
(Melbourne: Oxford University Press, 1976), pp. 61–2.

Strikingly, this hostility extended to indigenous forms of land use, that is, to the varieties of pastoralism and cultivation practised by African and Asian communities in territories recently colonized by Europeans. Pastoralists were accused of over-stocking and careless grazing practices, peasants of short-sightedness in their use of water and timber, but particular opprobrium was reserved for swidden or shifting agriculturists. Swidden farmers worked forest areas in rotation, burning and felling a patch of woodland before cultivating the soil for a few years, then moving on to the next patch: returning to the area originally felled once it had been fully reclaimed by forests, to start afresh this rotational cycle of fire, cultivation and fallowing. Although it had been successfully practised for generations, and sustained the economy of hill communities across large parts of Africa and Asia, to the European eye swidden cultivation epitomized indolence, instability and especially wastefulness, intensifying soil erosion and destroying forest areas that could perhaps be put to better use. Representative here are these remarks, dating from the 1860s, of a British forest officer on the Baigas of central India, a tribe that lived in valuable forests that the newly established Forest Department wished to take over. The officer wrote of this community of swidden farmers that they were 'the most terrible enemy to the forests we have anywhere in the hills.' It was sad 'to see the havoc that has been made among the forests by the Baiga axes.' In some areas 'the hills have been swept clean of forests for miles; in others, the Baiga marks are tall, blackened, charred stems standing in hundreds among the green forests'—it was 'really difficult to believe that so few people could sweep the face of the earth so clear of timber as they have done.'

However, scientific conservation was an ideology that was at once apocalyptic and redemptive. It did not hark back to an imagined past, but looked to reshape the present with the aid of reason and science. For rational planning would ensure that the 'great error' of waste—whether caused by settlers, native farmers, or industrialists—could be done away with, and a more efficient and sustainable system put in place. This could only be brought about by the state, the one body capable of taking a long-term view. For the profit motive was incompatible with conservation; with both individuals and enterprises being notoriously short-sighted, the state had to assume the responsibility for managing resources such as forests and water. Individuals and corporations came and went but the government, wrote the founder of the United States Forest Service, Gifford Pinchot, 'is not mortal. Men die but the Government lives on. The forests, like the race, must live on also. And the government alone can have, and does have, the continuity of purpose without which, in the long run, the forests cannot be saved.'

The opposition to private control was by no means an argument for locking up resources. It was, rather, a precondition for wise use. To quote Pinchot again, 'the job was not to stop the ax, but to regulate its use.' Likewise, the first head of the U.S. Bureau of Fisheries noted that 'while we are aiming to prevent the depletion of the great resources with which our country has been blessed, it follows logically that these resources must not be permitted to lie in a state of unproductive idleness.' The 'real problem of conservation,' he continued, 'is plainly a problem of efficient development and utilization.' That was a specific aim baldly stated: but men like Gifford Pinchot were also prone to identify their ideology with all that was good and noble in the human condition. In an essay published in the magazine *American Forests*, Pinchot wrote that Conservation

> is the wise and far-sighted use of all the things—natural, artificial, and spiritual—which men require upon this earth. . . . Conservation is as wide as the earth itself, as inclusive as the needs and interests of humanity upon the earth. It is far too great a question, therefore, to be included within the bounds of any single government department . . . It is the background, the spirit, and the strength of the progressive movement in American public life. It is the forward-looking point of view. It is the signboard on the road to a greater and better America.

Other conservationists were generally less lyrical, defining their faith more modestly in terms of its abhorrence of waste and its emphasis on wise use. These were embodied in the definition of conservation as 'the greatest good of the greatest number *for the longest time*,' this last phrase giving a distinctive twist to the ideals of utilitarian philosophy. The credo of scientific conservation was early and authoritatively expressed in George Perkins Marsh's *Man and Nature*, a book which drew upon the author's varied professional experience—as farmer, timber merchant, fish commissioner, plenipotentiary and Congressman—and his wide travels through North America and Europe. Recent scholarship has suggested that the strong and at times almost hysterical condemnation of peasants and pioneers by foresters and soil conservationists stemmed in good part from a competition for territory, with the conservationist aiming to take over, under state auspices, land or forests controlled by rival groups. Marsh himself was not interested in power; his language was sober rather than choleric, but his conclusions were equally disturbing. Taking a global view, he remarked that

Man has too long forgotten that the earth was given to him for usufruct alone, not for consumption, still less for profligate waste...There are parts of Asia Minor, of Northern Africa, of Greece, and even of Alpine Europe, where the operation of causes set in action by man has brought the face of the earth to a desolation almost as complete as that of the moon...The earth is fast becoming an unfit home for its noblest inhabitant, and another era of equal human crime and human improvidence...would reduce it to such a condition of impoverished productiveness, of shattered surface, of climatic excess, as to threaten the deprivation, barbarism, and perhaps even extinction of the species.

David Lowenthal, Marsh's biographer, writes that through the Vermonter's studies 'History revealed man as the architect of his own misfortune, but when the processes of nature were better understood, foresight and technical skill might reverse the decline.' In Marsh's view man was an agent of destruction as well as regeneration, with the potential, as he so beautifully put it, to be a 'restorer of disturbed harmonies.' For the history of early modern Europe had shown quite clearly that judicious intervention and systematic management could rehabilitate degraded forests, thereby arresting soil erosion, helping to regulate the flow of streams and rivers, and (not least) assuring a steady supply of wood for the economy. As Marsh wrote in the preface to his great work, 'my purpose is rather to make practical suggestions than to indulge in theoretical speculations.' Pre-eminent here was the need for public ownership of forests and water, resources so vital to the social and economic life of the nation. In his view, concessional grants to individuals and companies, while an attractive option in the short term, 'may become highly injurious to the public interest for years later:' an outcome he thought unlikely were these resources securely under state control. Marsh's insights, writes Lowenthal, were to 'become the guiding principles behind American conservation policy,' to be embodied, in time, in such institutions as the United States Forest Service and the Bureau of Reclamation.

The poet and critic Matthew Arnold said of Marsh that he was 'that *rara avis*, a really well-bred and trained American,' the characteristically English note of condescension barely masking what was well-considered and well-merited praise. But Marsh was also a genuine internationalist, who sought to influence the New World through the example of the Old, and whose work, in turn, was read and admired as far afield as India and Australia (and also in Russia, where his book had appeared in translation as early as 1866). Appositely, the Vermont conservationist spent his last days in a forestry school in the mountains above Florence, talking with students and walking among the firs. When he died there, on July 23, 1882, his body was draped in an American flag, but his coffin was carried down the hill by the Italian students, to be finally buried in a Protestant cemetery in Rome. In life, as in death, George Perkins Marsh epitomized the internationalism of scientific conservation, the movement of which he was such an outstanding exemplar.

THE GLOBAL REACH
OF SCIENTIFIC FORESTRY

Scientific forestry, the oldest and most influential strand in the conservation movement, had its origins in late medieval Europe. By the end of the nineteenth century, however, it had moved steadily outward to embrace much of the globe. France was a pioneer, introducing a Forest Code in the fourteenth century and a stricter forest ordinance in 1669, both initiatives aimed at regulating wood production for the navy. But by the eighteenth century, Germany had clearly emerged as the front-runner in the field.

The ascendancy of German forest science was a consequence of the quantitative methods developed there to estimate growing stock and yield. In large, powerful kingdoms such as Frederick the Great's Prussia, forestry officials reaped the benefits of a centralized administration which enabled the close supervision of state forests. In refining techniques of sustained-yield management, foresters moved from an area-based approach to a more reliable yield-based system. In the former case, foresters estimated the mature age of a tree species, then divided up the forest into areas whose number equalled this age (in years): on the assumption that equal areas yielded equal amounts of wood, the harvest of one patch annually would not dip into forest capital. Over time, this was replaced by a system based more directly on estimates of the volume and weight of trees of different ages. By carefully studying growth patterns on experimental plots, silviculturalists developed standard 'yield tables' for different species which computed, with a fair degree of accuracy, the wood mass of individual trees as well as of whole stands. These numbers, adjusted for varying soil and moisture conditions, then formed the basis of sustained-yield forestry.

To quote the historian Henry E. Lowood, 'Theories, practices and instructional models from Germany provided the starting point for every national effort in forest science and management until the end of the nineteenth century.' German foresters were mercenaries as well as missionaries, enthusiastically traveling abroad to promote

and propagate methods that had successfully stabilized the forest economy of their land. Throughout Europe, in Austria, Poland, Russia,
Finland, Sweden, even in France—close neighbor, old enemy, and
forestry pioneer itself—forest schools and departments were established on the German model and very often with German technical
support.

German experts also set up forestry establishments in their own
colonies and, perhaps more surprisingly, in colonies controlled by
rival European powers as well. When the Dutch wished to systemati-
cally exploit the teak forests of Java, they could only turn to Germans for advice. From 1849 till the early decades of this century, a
stream of German experts arrived to help the Dutch colonies institute a forest regime, based on strict state control. The foresters' brief
was to harvest teak for the construction of roads, railways, and for
the growing export trade—teak being a high-quality wood plundered
for making furniture to adorn European drawing rooms. Likewise,
the Indian Forest Department was serenely guided, for its first half
century, by three successive German Inspectors General of Forest:
Dietrich Brandis, Wilhelm Schlich, and Bertold von Ribbentrop. The
Germans took on a wide array of tasks seen as essential for successful forest administration: the reservation of forest areas to the state,
by curtailing or extinguishing rights exercised by village communities; dividing up these reserves into territories controlled by individual officers; identifying valuable species and studying their growth
curves; and finally, establishing schools and laboratories for further-
ing research and education. In time, British officers trained by Brandis
and company emerged as forest internationalists in their own right,
with officials of the Indian Forest Service helping to set up forest departments in West and East Africa, in South East Asia, and in New
Zealand.

One of the most remarkable of these German forestry missionaries was Ferdinand Müeller, a graduate of the University of Kiel
appointed Government Botanist of the Australian province of Victoria
in 1852. Over a forty-year period Mueller used the varied fora of the
government commission, the scientific seminar and the newspaper
column in awakening the Australian public to the destruction of forests which provided pit props for their mines, charcoal for their railway engines and, indirectly, water for their rivers. Unusually for a
forester, Mueller used ethical and esthetic arguments in conjunction
with the more familiar utilitarian ones. In an address of June 1871 to
the Technological Museum in Melbourne, he urged that the forest be
seen

as an heritage given to us by nature, not for spoil or to devastate, but to be wisely used, reverently honoured, and carefully maintained. I regard the forests as a gift, entrusted to any of us only for transient care during a short space of time, to be surrendered to posterity again as an unimpaired property, with increased riches and augmented blessings, to pass as a sacred patrimony from generation to generation.

The German experience also deeply stamped the evolution of North American forestry. A Prussian forester, Bernhard Fernow, was in 1879 appointed the first chief of the Division of Forestry in the Federal Government; he went on to set up forestry schools at the universities of Cornell and Toronto. When a full-fledged forest service was created in 1900, its first head was a home-grown American, Gifford Pinchot, the scion of a distinguished Pennsylvania Republican family who ended up as governor of his home state. But Pinchot himself always maintained that his mentor was Dietrich Brandis, the German scientist who set up the Indian Forest Department. When, in the 1880s, the American decided to make a career in forestry, he made a pilgrimage to Bonn, where Brandis lived in retirement. Brandis took charge of Pinchot's education, continuing to advise him after his return to the United States. In his autobiography, *Breaking New Ground*, Pinchot generously acknowledged this debt. 'Measured by any standard, Brandis was the first of living foresters,' he wrote, who 'had done great work as a pioneer, and had made Forestry to be where there was none before. In a word, he had accomplished on the other side of the world [in India] what I might hope to have a hand in doing in America.' The impact of Brandis on Pinchot, and the more general influence of German forestry on American forestry, are illustrated in the *box*.

Gifford Pinchot also helped found a forestry school at Yale University which rapidly established itself as a world leader in forestry research and education. Fittingly, it was the Yale University Press which, in 1938, published the first historical survey of the significance and impact of German forestry. The author, a reputed German silviculturist named Franz Heske, celebrated his country's experience as a 'shining example for forestry in all the world.' After having transformed their 'depleted, abused woods' into 'well-managed forests with steadily increasing yields,' German foresters, working at home and overseas, had made it

considerably easier for the rest of the world to pursue a similar course, because the attainable goal is now known, at least in principle. The sponsors of sustained-yield in countries where forestry is still new can find in the results of this large-scale German experiment a strong support in their battle with those who know nothing, who believe nothing, and who wish to do nothing [to protect forests]. This experiment and its outcome have rendered inestimable service in the cause of a regulated, planned development and use of the earth's raw materials, which will be an essential feature of the coming organic world economy.

AMERICA LOOKS TO EUROPE

Two Chiefs of the United States Forest Service outline their country's debt to Germany and Germans.

1. We see the need of curbing individualistic exploitation and we are looking towards the future with justified apprehension. In this situation we instinctively turn to the experience of older countries. . . . In Germany the conflict between public interest and private right is resolved by the concept of the dependence of the individual on the nation as a whole, 'Gemeinnutz geht vor Eigennutz.' In no other framework could the crowded nations of Europe maintain their national well-being. This tenet of totality is the growth of centuries of sacrifice and struggle. It has gained a perspective in which the future becomes a fixed reality. In German forestry policy this concept is expressed in what foresters call sustained-yield management. It is what Dr Heske calls it, an example for all the world.

2. His connection . . . with the English students led Sir Dietrich [Brandis] very naturally to take charge of American students who came to Europe to study. Taking charge of a student meant with him not merely to advise as to the general course of study, but also to require bi-weekly reports, and to read and to criticize them, to send long letters written in longhand to each of us from time to time, and in every detail to try, with a never-ending patience, enthusiasm and generosity, to see that each of us got from his work exactly what he came for. This was done for me, then for Graves, then for Price, Olmsted, Sherrad and many others. Sir Dietrich thus had a guiding hand in shaping many of the men whose fortune it became afterwards to shape the general policy of forestry in the United States.

Source: 1. Henry S. Graves, 'Preface,' in Franz Heske, *German Forestry* (New Haven: Yale University Press, 1938), pp. xvii–xviii.
2. Gifford Pinchot, 'Sir Dietrich Brandis,' *Proceedings of the Society of American Foresters*, volume 3, number 1, 1908, pp. 58–9.

A forestry pioneer trained in France rather than Germany was the Mexican Miguel Angel de Quevedo. Born in 1862, Quevedo took a bachelor's degree in Bordeaux before moving to the Ecole Polytechnique in Paris to study hydraulic engineering. Here one of his teachers told him that an engineer not instructed in forestry was 'deficient, an ignoramus who will make grave mistakes.' The lesson came home most forcefully when Quevedo returned to Mexico in 1887, and began work as a hydraulic engineer. Supervising a drainage project outside the capital, Mexico City, he came to understand the impact of deforestation in the hills on flooding in the plains below. He then spent a decade as a consultant to various hydro-electric companies, studying afresh how forest cover, or its disappearance, had an impact on water flow and rates of sedimentation.

Quevedo's public debut as a forestry campaigner came at a 1901 conference on climate and meteorology. Here he spoke out on the need for a nation-wide law to protect and replenish Mexico's fast-depleting forests. He then started a lobbying group, the Junta Central de Bosques: this promoted parks and tree nurseries in the cities, and compiled inventories of forest cover in different districts. In 1917 he persuaded the new post-revolutionary government to insert a clause in the Constitution, which read: 'The nation shall always have the right to impose on private property the rules dictated by the public interest and to regulate the use of natural elements, susceptible to appropriation so as to distribute equitably the public wealth and to safeguard its conservation.'

In 1922 Quevedo founded the Mexican Forestry Society to more effectively 'clamor against the silence of our country against the national suicide that signifies the ruin of the forest and the scorn of our tree protector.' Quevedo and his society were instrumental in the passing, at last, of a national forest act in 1926. By now, his work had come to the attention of Mexico's new President, Lazaro Cardenas, a progressive reformer already known for his interest in land reform and workers' rights. In 1935 Cardenas created a Department of Forestry, Fish and Game. Quevedo was appointed its first commissioner, an appointment, as one of his followers remarked, which 'constituted the synthesis and crowning achievement of the great work in defense and propagation of our natural resources that the wise investigator, the noble apostle, the pure spirit, Miguel Angel de Quevedo has undertaken during his life.'

Quevedo's recent biographer, Lane Simonian, likewise refers to him as 'Mexico's apostle of the tree.' He was certainly a remarkable man, in energy and foresight fully the equal of other and, thus far, better-known conservationists from other lands. Quevedo shared with these contemporaries a hostility to peasants, whom he held to be chiefly responsible for the destruction of his country's forests. He also tended to oscillate between exuberant optimism, foreseeing

a future when scientists would finally be in charge, and bleak pessi-
mism, in case his technically equipped visionaries were not placed in
positions of power and influence. The following quote, from 1939,
captures him in the latter mood, in despair after forty years of mostly
unsuccessful preaching and proselytizing:

> Each day the Mexican forest problem becomes graver: the large woods
> are being depleted at an alarming rate, the production of chicle diminishes
> notably year by year, the hardwoods and even firewood cannot be
> obtained in regions once classified as heavily forested. Everywhere one
> observes forests impoverished and ruined by greed and thoughtfulness
> and almost we can claim that Mexico is heading for drought.
>
> [translated by Lane Simonian]

THE BALANCE SHEET OF SCIENTIFIC FORESTRY

The actual experience of scientific forestry was quite often at odds
with its professed aims and supposed achievements. Especially in the
colonies, it followed a 'custodial' approach, with the strengthening
of state control having as its corollary the denial of customary rights
of user exercised by peasant and tribal communities. For the acres
and acres of woodland taken over by the state were by no means
pristine, untouched forests; rather, they had been controlled and used
by humans down the centuries. Peasants and pastoralists, swidden
cultivators and wood-working artisans, all looked upon the forest as
a provider of their basic means of subsistence: the source of fuel for
cooking, grass for livestock, leaf for manure, timber for homes and
plows, bamboos for baskets, land for extending cultivation, herbs
for curing ailments, and so on. When access to these resources was
restricted by the creation of strictly protected government reserves,
escalating conflict between local communities and forest departments
was the inevitable outcome.

In South Asia, where the history of scientific forestry has perhaps been most fully documented, the forest department quickly became a reviled arm of the colonial state. When a comprehensive
Indian Forest Act was enacted in 1878—to supersede a preliminary
Act of 1865—the government was warned, by a dissenting official,
that the new legislation would leave 'a deep feeling of injustice and
resentment amongst our agricultural communities;' indeed, the act
might 'place in antagonism to Government every class whose support is desired and essential to the object in view [i.e. forest conser-
vation], from the Zamindar [landlord] to the Hill Toda [tribal].' These

words were far-sighted, for once the act was in place, peasant and tribal groupings resisted the operations of the Forest Department in all kinds of ways: through arson, breaches of the forest law, attacks on officials and on government property, and quite often, through co-ordinated and collective social movements aimed at restoring local control over forests. These rebellions formed part of broader nationalist upsurges; sometimes engulfing thousands of square miles, they were quelled only by the superior firepower of the colonial army and police.

A flavor of the sentiments behind these militant and enduring protests is contained in some remarks of the nineteenth-century social reformer, Jotiba Phule. Writing in 1881, Phule captured the transformations that the forest department had wrought in the Indian countryside. 'In the old days,' remarked the reformer,

> small landholders who could not subsist on cultivation alone used to eat wild fruits like figs and [berries] and sell the leaves and flowers of the flame of the forest and the mahua tree. They could also depend on the village ground to maintain one or two cows and two or four goats, thereby living happily in their own ancestral villages. However, the cunning European employees of our motherly government have used their foreign brains to erect a great superstructure called the forest department. With all the hills and undulating areas as also the fallow lands and grazing grounds brought under the control of this forest department, the livestock of the poor farmers do not even have place to breathe anywhere on the surface of the earth.
>
> [translated from the Marathi by Madhav Gadgil]

These contemporary *social* criticisms of scientific forestry (see also quotes in *box*) have now been joined by retrospective *environmental* ones. Recent work by ecologists suggests that, at least in the tropics, sustained-yield forestry has been honored mostly in the breach. Tropical forests are very diverse in their species composition, quite unlike the species-poor temperate woodlands where scientific forestry was first formulated and, for the most part, successfully applied. In Northern Europe, a single species of pine might dominate large areas of forest; a situation far removed from the tropical humid forests of Asia and Africa, in one acre of which dozens of tree species co-exist along with hundreds of plant varieties in the understorey, not to speak of thousands of micro-organisms and animals of many shapes and sizes. In South and South-east Asia, an additional complicating factor is the monsoon, the two or three months of torrential rain which quickly wash away soil exposed by logging, thus rendering regeneration extraordinarily difficult. In such circumstances, it is

The long straight lines of scientific forestry: an eucalyptus plantation in Goa, Southern India.

SOURCE Photo by M. D. Subhas Chandran

highly questionable whether sustained-yield forestry on the European model can be successfully practised, a skepticism that is borne out by the record. In India, for instance, 130 years of state forest management have left the forests in much poorer condition than they were when scientific forestry first made its appearance. Twenty-two per cent of India's land mass is still controlled by the forest department, but less than half of this has tree cover on it: proof of the failures of German forestry to successfully replicate itself in the tropics.

PEASANTS VERSUS THE FOREST DEPARTMENT

In 1913 the Government of Madras appointed a Commission to investigate grievances against the forest administration. Offered here are two exchanges with the Commission, one with a group of ryots (peasants), the other with an individual landholder identified by name. The conversations reveal the sharp opposition between scientific foresters and the interests of the rural community.

Committee	: What is your next grievance?
Ryots	: We have no firewood; and are not given permits for them.
Committee	: Are you willing to pay for permits for firewood?
Ryots	: No; it has not been the custom up till now. There are only three or four rich ryots and all the rest are poor and cannot pay for fuel. We pray that we may be given the grants.
Committee	: At present what do you burn?
Ryots	: We use cow-dung cakes . . . We want more manure leaves.
Committee	: Do you always use them?
Ryots	: When the land was a [commons], we used to get leaves for manure, sixteen years ago.
Committee	: You do not get them now?
Ryots	: Occasionally one or two men who can afford it send their men to distant places to get leaves.
Committee	: What are your difficulties about the forests?
Timma Reddy	: There are two temples on the top of the hill . . . There is worship there every week. There are many devotees. If ryots go there, the forest subordinates trouble them and they do not go even to the temple. If we do not worship in any year, tanks will not get supply of water.

Committee	: Did you worship this year?
Timma Reddy	: Yes. A case was also made against us. While the God was being taken along the path, some trees were said to have been injured and the District Forest Officer inquired and let us off. . . . We worship every year. Instead of worshipping the God there, the ryots have to worship the forest subordinates.
Committee	: Did you not represent to the District Forest Officer?
Timma Reddy	: Once we went to worship the God and a case was made against my brother that he went for hunting. The District Forest Officer charged us for trial in the Taluk Magistrate's Court. There we were acquitted. Even if we go to the D.F.O., we thought we will not have justice. So we do not go to him.

Source: Atluri Murali, 'Whose Trees? Forest Practices and Local Communities in Andhra, 1600–1922,' in David Arnold and Ramachandra Guha, editors, *Nature, Culture, Imperialism: Essays on the Environmental History of South Asia* (New Delhi: Oxford University Press), pp. 106, 110.

One Asian country that has not followed European models—in this as in so many other respects—is Japan, also, and not coincidentally, a country that never came under colonial rule. Independent of, and at least as early as in Germany, Japanese scientists had developed skilled methods of regenerative forestry that helped stabilize the forest cover and mountain slopes of their islands. The historian Conrad Totman notes that between 1590 and 1660 Japanese farmers and timber merchants 'devastated much of their forest land and seemed to be in the process of pressing the archipelago beyond endurance.' Disaster was forestalled by a mix of negative and positive interventions; the former aimed at restricting and regulating tree-felling so as to assist natural regeneration, the latter at more actively enhancing tree cover through plantations, especially of conifers. Large tracts of woodland owned by temples and shrines were also sequestered by the central government, to be worked on rotations of a hundred years and more. Meanwhile, a proliferation of books and pamphlets authored by officials and intellectuals urged the public to help the government protect forests and pass on their patrimony to later generations. As Totman observes, the concerns of these writers were emphatically practical, affirming not a mystic ecological consciousness—of the

kind looked for by recent Western enthusiasts of Japanese Zen Buddhism—but, rather, highlighting the very real dangers of soil erosion
and resource shortages that deforestation would give rise to. An
official of the Akita district wrote, in the early seventeenth century, that 'The treasure of the realm is the treasure of the mountains
[i.e. soil and water]. When all the trees are cut and gone, however,
their value will be nil. Before all is lost, proper care must be taken.
Destitution of the mountains will result in destitution of the realm.'
This is a succinct statement of the ideology of scientific conservation, apocalyptic at one level, holding out the hope of redemption at
another.

4

The Growth of the Wilderness Idea

I shift now to a third variety of environmentalism, the conservation of wild species and wild habitats. The formal history of wilderness conservation is little more than a century old, but viewed more broadly this movement has an ancient lineage. On the one side are popular traditions of 'sacred groves,' patches of forest worshipped as the home of deities and protected from human interference, that are to be found in all non-Christian cultures: Hindu Nepal, Buddhist Thailand, those parts of Africa that retain their ancestral religions. On the other side were elite feudal traditions of 'hunting preserves'—prevalent in Norman England, Qing China and Mughal India—where animal species such as the tiger and the deer were reserved for the exclusive pleasure of lords and kings, with peasants and commoners banned from the hunt and sometimes from the preserve itself. However, my focus here is on the distinctively modern traditions of nature conservation, the growth of the wilderness idea in the decades since the establishment of the first national park in the western United States during the latter half of the nineteenth century.

CONSERVATION IN THE COLONIES

We live in a time of international environmental conferences: seminars of atmospheric scientists, struggling to make sense of the dynamics of climate change; meetings of heads of state, putting their signatures to this or that treaty to protect biodiversity; communions of social activists, exchanging notes on how best to mobilize public opinion to resist environmental degradation.

These meetings have become more frequent in recent years, with the revolution in communications and the growing ease with which people now talk or move back and forth across the continents. But which was the first-ever 'international' environmental conference? It took place in the distant year 1900, in the city of London, and its topic was the protection of the wildlife of Africa. Characteristically for the times, there were no Africans present, the delegates to the meeting being the foreign ministers of the European colonial powers who then controlled the continent: France, Germany, Belgium, Italy, Spain, Portugal, and pre-eminently, Great Britain.

Convened by the British Foreign Office, the London conference was spurred by the massive destruction of African wildlife by European hunters in the preceding decades. For young men serving in the outposts of empire, hunting was the preferred form of recreation, offering trophies scarcely to be found at home. As one colonial official candidly remarked in 1857, 'the main attraction of India lay in the splendid field it offered for the highest and noblest order of sport, in the pursuit of the wild and savage denizens of its forests and jungles, its mountains and groves:' hunting here was, indeed, a 'welcome change from the boredom of shooting seals in the Shetland Isles.' India boasted the tiger and the Asian elephant, but Africa offered greater opportunities still. Through the nineteenth century, European soldiers, officials, missionaries and travellers relentlessly hunted anything that moved: elephant, lion, leopard, cheetah, zebra, antelope, or wildebeest. By the turn of the century, as *The Times* of London recorded, it was

> necessary to go far into the interior to find the nobler forms of antelope and still further if the hunter wants to pursue the elephant, the rhinoceros, or the giraffe. It is perfectly clear that very soon those animals, unless something is done to prevent their extermination, will be stamped out as completely as the dodo.

The parties to the London conference of 1900 signed a 'Convention for the Preservation of Animals, Birds and Fish in Africa.' Although the title indicates a grand sweep, in point of fact the conservation measures introduced were rather modest. Only a few endangered species were accorded complete protection: these included the gorilla, the giraffe, and the chimpanzee. For some other threatened species, such as the elephant and the gazelle, hunters were given licenses which limited the numbers that could be shot and prohibited the shooting of infants and pregnant females. Ironically, some species were classified as 'vermin,' deemed dangerous to men and cattle, and their killing was expressly encouraged. Bounties were thus offered for the shooting of the lion and the leopard—among the most cherished of wild animals from today's vantage point.

The London meeting was soon followed by the establishment of the first multinational conservation society. This was the 'Society for the Preservation of the Fauna of the Empire,' started in 1903 to halt the destruction of wild animals in the British colonies. The Society had local chapters across a wide swathe of Asia and Africa: dominated everywhere by hunters turned conservationists, it was known 'on account of its nucleus of elderly big game hunters as the Repentant Butchers Club.'

Through the colonies, wildlife conservation followed a set pattern. The first step was to moderate demand by specifying closed seasons when animals could not be shot, and issuing licenses, the possession of which alone allowed hunting. The second step was to designate particular species as 'protected.' The third step was to designate specified territories as 'game reserves' meant exclusively for animals, where logging, mining and agriculture were prohibited or restricted. The final and most decisive step was the establishment of national parks, which gave sanctity to entire habitats, not merely to animal species dwelling within them (see *box*).

In Southern Africa, the progress of conservation was linked to the development of a distinct settler identity. As English and Dutch colonists settled in for the long haul, identifying with Africa and turning their backs on their country of origin, the preservation of landscapes became synonymous with the preservation of the national spirit. Prominent Afrikaaner politicians, such as Paul Kruger and Jan Smuts, called for the creation of parks and sanctuaries so that the children and grandchildren of the pioneers could see the veld 'just as the Voortrekkers saw it.' The creation of reserves was thus dictated by sentiment as well as science, to simultaneously allow space for wild species and to affirm a shared human past. In neighboring Southern Rhodesia, where the English dominated, the grave in the Matopos hills of the great imperialist Cecil Rhodes became the nucleus of a national park extending over 45,000 acres.

Where did the African fit into all this? To be precise, nowhere. The white settler identified with the land but not with the men and women who had dwelt there long before their arrival. As the historians Jane Carruthers and Terence Ranger have pointed out, wildlife conservation cemented a union between the Dutch and the English in southern Africa, but it also consolidated, on the whole, white domination over the majority black population. In game reserves Africans were barred from hunting, while in national parks they were excluded altogether, forcibly dispossessed of their land if it fell within the boundaries of a designated sanctuary. Conservation was even viewed as 'part of the white man's necessary burden to save the nation's natural heritage from African despoilation.' But this was a conveniently ahistorical belief which glossed over the butchery of European hunting in the early decades of colonialism. If there was indeed a 'crisis of African wildlife,' this crisis had been created by the white man's gun and rifle, not the native spear and sling shot.

AND WHY A NATIONAL PARK?

In 1916 a Games Reserves Commission outlined the reasons for the creation of National Parks in South Africa. Note however that terms such as 'the general public' and 'the town dweller' refer exclusively to one race only, that is, white, and for the most part also to one sex, that is, male.

We think that . . . greater facilities should be offered to scientists, naturalists, and the general public to make themselves acquainted with a portion of their country which should be of the greatest natural interest for the following reasons:

(i) Here one may view and study conditions once generally obtaining throughout large areas of the Union, but which, owing to the advance of civilisation, are now rapidly disappearing and must eventually disappear altogether.

(ii) As a training ground for the scientific student, whether in botany, zoology, or other directions, the area is unequalled.

(iii) It is becoming more and more difficult for the town dweller to gain knowledge of the natural conditions of the country, and with the gradual extinction of game and other animals that is steadily going on, even to see the fauna of the country other than in the sophisticated surroundings of a zoological collection.

(iv) Here and nowhere better can the natural surroundings and habits of South African fauna be really studied, unaffected as the animals are by the instinctive dread of the huntsman, which in other parts of the country tend completely to alter their habits.

Source: Jane Carruthers, *The Kruger National Park: A Social and Political History* (Pietermaritzburg: University of Natal Press, 1995), p. 56.

Poster encouraging visitors to a national park in South Africa.

SOURCE Jane Carruthers, The Kruger National Park (*University of Natal Press.*)

WILDERNESS THINKING IN AMERICA

The first national park created anywhere was Yellowstone,
By now there are a thousand such parks spread across the gl
United States has itself created what is generally regarded to be the
best-managed system of national parks in the world. It is also in the
U.S. that intellectuals and thinkers have pondered most deeply on
what the wilderness has meant for the nourishment of the human
spirit.

The background to wilderness conservation was the despoliation
of the American continent by the westward movement of European settlers. In an essay published in the July 1897 number of the
Atlantic Monthly, the California writer John Muir captured the environmental destruction caused by the pioneer's axe and fire, his corn
fields and his cattle and sheep herds. Muir wrote stirringly of the
past, present and possible future of the

American forests! the glory of the world! Surveyed thus from the east
to the west, from the north to the south, they are rich beyond thought,
immortal, immeasurable, enough and to spare for every feeding,
sheltering beast and bird, insect and son of Adam; and nobody need
have cared had there been no pines in Norway, no cedars and deodars
on Lebanon and the Himalayas, no vine-clad selvas in the basin of the
Amazon. With such variety, harmony, and triumphant exuberance, even
nature, it would seem, might have rested content with the forests of
North America, and planted no more.

So they appeared a few centuries ago when they were rejoicing in
wildness. The Indians with stone axes could do them no more harm
than could gnawing beavers or browsing moose. Even the fires of the
Indian and the fierce shattering lightning seemed to work together only
for good in clearing spots here and there for smooth garden prairies, and
openings for sunflowers seeking the light. But when the steel axe of the
white man rang out in the startled air, the doom [of the forest] was
sealed. Every tree heard the bodeful sound, and pillars of smoke gave
the sign in the sky.

I suppose we need not go mourning the buffaloes. In the nature of
things they had to give place to better cattle, though the change might
have been made without barbarous wickedness. Likewise, many of
nature's five hundred kinds of wild trees had to make way for orchards
and cornfields. In the settlement and civilization of the country, bread
more than timber or beauty was wanted; and in the blindness of hunger,
the early settlers, claiming Heaven as their guide, regarded God's trees
as only a larger kind of pernicious weed, extremely hard to get rid of.

Accordingly, with no eye to the future, these pious destroyers waged interminable forest wars; chips flew thick and fast; trees in their beauty fell crashing by millions, smashed to confusion, and the smoke of their burning has been rising to heaven [for] more than two hundred years. After the Atlantic coast from Maine to Georgia had been mostly cleared and scorched into melancholy ruins, the overflowing multitudes of bread and money seekers poured over the Alleghanies into the fertile middle West, spreading ruthless devastation ever wider and further over the rich valley of the Mississippi and the vast shadowy pine region about the Great Lakes. Thence still westward the invading horde of destroyers called settlers made its fiery way over the broad Rocky Mountains, felling and burning more fiercely than ever, until at last it has reached the wild side of the continent, and entered the last of the great aboriginal forests on the shores of the Pacific.

This is a crisp if starkly chilling summation of the ecological history of eighteenth- and nineteenth-century America. Fortunately, by the time Muir penned these words public opinion had been sufficiently stirred to try and protect the 'aboriginal forest' that remained. As he noted with relief and pleasure, lovers of the landscape, 'bewailing its baldness, are now crying aloud, "Save what is left of the forest!" Clearing has surely now gone far enough; soon timber will be scarce, and not a grove will be left to rest in or pray in.'

John Muir himself was one who shouted loudest, longest, and most effectively. Born in the Scottish town of Dunbar in 1838, he moved with his family to Wisconsin when a young boy. Here he grew up on a pioneer's farm, with an interest in botany and geology and an aptitude for things mechanical. After a desultory year or two at the University of Wisconsin, he left his home for the road, travelling through Canada before walking a thousand miles down to the Gulf of Mexico. Reaching San Francisco in March 1868, he settled in California, making repeated and extended forays into the Sierra mountains. Within a decade he had become known as a writer and lecturer, speaking out on the need to save what remained of the Western wilderness. In 1892 he founded the Sierra Club, which has since been the most influential conservation society in the career of American environmentalism.

Like Mahatma Gandhi, John Muir was not a systematic thinker: his ideas are scattered through his articles and speeches; they are not to be found in one, single, authoritative text. Yet there is no question that—like Gandhi—he was a thinker far ahead of his time. He knew well the economic rationale for forest protection—to supply a steady supply of timber, to prevent soil erosion, and to regulate the flow of

John Muir, at his desk, c. 1897.

SOURCE Muir Papers, University of the Pacific, Stockton, California, here taken from Stephen Fox, The American Conservation Movement *(University of Wisconsin Press.)*

water in the rivers—yet he also believed passionately in an independent, non-utilitarian rationale for preserving the wild. In an early meeting of the Sierra Club, he pointed out that

> any kind of forest on the flank of the Sierra would be of inestimable
> value as a cover for the irrigating streams. But in our forests we have not
> only a perfect cover, but also the most attractive and interesting trees
> in every way, and of the highest value, spiritual and material, so that even
> the angels of heaven might well be eager to come down and camp in their
> leafy temples!

Brought up a devout Christian, the son of an evangelical preacher,
Muir came to embrace a mystical pantheism somewhat at odds with
his received religious tradition. Christian doctrine puts man in a position of dominance over the rest of creation, but for Muir, as one
admirer noted, 'cliff, air, cloud, flower, tree, bird and beast—all these
were manifestations of a unifying God.' For him every species had
its own honored place in the scheme of Nature. Man thought himself the master of the Universe, but Muir insisted that

> Nature's object in making animals and plants might possibly be first of
> all the happiness of each one of them, not the creation of all for the
> happiness of one. Why should man value himself as more than a small
> part of the one great unit of creation? And what creature of all that the
> Lord has taken the pains to make is not essential to the completeness
> of that unit—the cosmos? The universe would be incomplete without
> man; but it would also be incomplete without the smallest trans-
> microscopic creature that dwells beyond our conceitful eyes and
> knowledge.

Muir wrote evocatively of landscapes, and lovingly of individual species too. The Sierra bear was for him 'the sequioa of the animals,' a
fellow rambler in the forest who was 'everywhere at home, harmonizing with the trees and rocks and shaggy chapparal.' The water ouzel
was a 'brave little singer on the wild mountain streams;' to see this
bird and love him was 'to look through a window into Nature's warm
heart.' To the city-dweller nature was distant at best, terrifying at
worst, but to Muir the forest and its diverse inhabitants were always
welcoming. When the philosopher Ralph Waldo Emerson visited
Yosemite, Muir tried in vain to take him to the wild. He wanted to
show Emerson the 'Sierra manifestations of God,' but the great man's
hangers-on, full of the 'indoor philosophy of Boston,' held him to
the hotels and approved trails. However, towards the end of his life
Muir was heartened to see growing numbers of city folk come out to

savor the glories of the Sierra. He saw that 'thousands of tired, nerve-shaken, over-civilized people are beginning to find out that going to the mountains is going home.' To Muir this was proof that 'wildness is a necessity; and that mountain peaks and [forest] reservations are useful not only as fountains of timber and irrigating rivers, but as fountains of life.'

In contrast to John Muir, for whom the Sierra was a second and occasionally a first home, these 'over-civilized' folk lived the year round in the cities and only seasoned their lives, a week at a time, with the wild. By the early twentieth century, growing urbanization had spawned a leisure industry which created a powerful social force for the preservation of wild areas. Muir might have wanted to protect Nature for its own sake, but the more humdrum pleasures of weekend camping and trekking played as influential a part in the creation of a national park system. As the historian Alfred Runte points out, the first reserve established on purely ecological grounds was the Everglades national park, created in 1934. Runte suggests that in fact several of the early national parks were created specifically to meet a rising surge of cultural nationalism. The apparent agelessness and sheer size of their mountains and forests provided, for the American intelligentsia, a substitute for the rich traditions of art and architecture that their country so conspicuously lacked. Unlike Europe, where the farmer and the shepherd carried in themselves the continuity of an ancient culture, there was no authentic heritage here of peasant life and traditions. Meanwhile, this land's indigenous inhabitants, the Native Americans, had been decimated in numbers and become degenerate in spirit. Into this void stepped the wilderness, which became, so to speak, *America's past*—a past to be mighty proud of. For if the Sierra redwoods had begun to grow before the birth of Christ, if the Rockies were twice as high as the Alps, and if compared to the Mississippi the Danube was a mere ditch, then this new nation could boast of a series of natural wonders vastly superior to the man-made artefacts, the churches, forts and paintings of Europe. In this sense, the monumental and unsurpassed scenery of the West provided American patriots with a way to answer Europe, the ancient civilization with respect to which they had a marked inferiority complex.

John Muir was himself a kind of ecological patriot, who believed that American forests were second to none: in their 'variety, harmony and triumphant exuberance' superior to the cedars of Lebanon, the deodars of the Himalaya, the selvas of the Amazon. But it is the ecological sensitivity rather than the patriotism which makes his a distinctive voice. Muir is rightly honored for his consideration for species other than the human, for his dogged insistence (see *box*) that nature had a right to be cared for regardless of any man's bank balance or any country's gross national product. He has become something of a cult figure for latter-day environmentalists, who worship him as a bearded prophet, alone in the wild, embattled and beleaguered, crying out against the forces of commerce and industry that would devastate nature. Just adjacent to John Muir in the pantheon of the wilderness movement is the man we now come to, Aldo Leopold.

HOW AND HOW NOT TO
REVERENCE NATURE

John Muir on the threats to nature, and how to forestall or work around them.

1. Travellers in the Sierra forests usually complain of the want of life. 'The trees,' they say, 'are fine, but the empty stillness is deadly; there are no animals to be seen, no birds. We have not heard a song in all the woods.' And no wonder! They go in large parties with miles and horses; they make a great noise; they are dressed in outlandish, unnatural colors; every animal shuns them. Even the frightened pines would run away if they could. But Nature lovers, devout, silent, open-eyed, looking and listening with love, find no lack of inhabitants in these mountain mansions, and they come to them gladly.

2. The battle we have fought, and are still fighting, for the forests [of the Sierra] is a part of the eternal conflict between right and wrong, and we cannot expect to see the end of it. . . . The smallest forest reserve, and the first I ever heard of, was in the Garden of Eden; and though its boundaries were drawn by the Lord, and embraced only one tree, yet even so moderate a reserve as this was attacked. And I doubt not, if only one of our grand trees on the Sierra were reserved as an example and type of all that is most noble and glorious in mountain trees, it would not be long before you would find a lumberman and a lawyer at the foot of it, eagerly proving by every law terrestrial and celestial that the tree must come down. So we must count on watching and striving for these trees, and should always be glad to find anything so surely good and noble to strive for.

Sources: 1. 'Among the Yosemite,' *The Atlantic Monthly*, December 1898, p. 751. 2. 'Address on the Sierra Forest Reservation,' *The Sierra Club Bulletin*, volume 1, number 7, 1896, p. 276.

Leopold was born in January 1887 into a family of cultured and highly educated German immigrants. He grew up amidst books and music, but also acquired an interest in the outdoors, inspired by his father, a keen hunter himself. Aldo went on to obtain a degree at the Yale School of Forestry, before joining the United States Forest Service in 1909. He worked in the Forest Service for a quarter of a century, mostly in the south-west. In 1933 he moved to a Professorship at the University of Wisconsin, dividing his time between the college campus and a small farm he had bought in the country.

In his career Leopold was to shift allegiance from one variety of environmentalism to another. Long years in the Forest Service, that showcase of scientific conservation, prepared him for a late emergence as a philosopher of nature, as what one colleague termed 'the Commanding General of the Wilderness Battle.' Posted in forest areas with plentiful populations of wild animals, Leopold developed a philosophy of 'game management' modelled closely on the principles of scientific forestry, with game replacing timber as the product which needed to be harvested on a 'sustained-yield' basis. But in time he came to appreciate the cultural and ecological significance of the wild, and from promoting 'game refuges' began urging that a portion of the National Forests be set aside as fully protected wilderness.

Leopold's move from the Forest Service to the University of Wisconsin was also a move from the tradition of Gifford Pinchot to the tradition of John Muir, and beyond (see quotes in *box*). In January 1935 he helped found the Wilderness Society, an autonomous pressure group that embraced both a philosophical credo—'an intelligent humility towards man's place in nature—and a practical program, the setting aside for posterity of wild areas as yet untouched by mining, industry, logging, roads and other such threats. Later the same year, Leopold went on a study tour of Germany, where he was dismayed by the artificialized systems of forest and game management, which had reduced the diversity found in nature in favour of a few select species. He remarked, of the mania for spruce, that 'never before or since have the forests of a whole nation been converted into a new species within a single generation.' The Germans, wrote Leopold in disgust, had 'taught the world to plant trees like cabbages.'

In *A Sand County Alamanac*, his chronicle of life on a Wisconsin farm, Leopold offered moving descriptions of the coming and passing of the seasons, the changes through the year in plant and animal life. The land he tilled formed part of the prairie where the buffalo had once roamed in large numbers. Characteristically, Leopold mourned not so much the great buffalo as the lowly Sulphium, a native weed being exterminated by the plow and the lawn mower. The disappearance of Sulphium, he remarked, was 'one little episode in the funeral

of the native flora, which in turn is one episode in the funeral of the
floras of the world.'

ALDO LEOPOLD CHANGES ALLEGIANCES

*Aldo Leopold moved from being a hard-nosed utilitarian conservationist
to a philosopher of ecological harmony and interdependence. These
quotes help mark the shift:*

1. A harmonious relation to land is more intricate, and of more
    consequence to civilization, than the historians of its progress seem
    to realize. Civilization is not, as they often assume, the enslavement
    of a stable and consistent earth. It is a state of mutual and
    interdependent cooperation between human animals, other animals,
    plants and soils, which may be disrupted at any moment by the failure
    of any of them.

2. The emergence of ecology has placed the economic biologist in a
    peculiar dilemma: with one hand, he points out the accumulated
    findings of his search for utility, or lack of utility, in this or that
    species; with the other he lifts the veil from a biota so complex, so
    conditioned by interwoven cooperations and competitions, that no
    man can say where utility begins or ends.

Source: 1. 'The Conservation Ethic,' *Journal of Forestry*, volume 31,
number 6, 1933, p. 635. 2. 'A Biotic View of Land,' *Journal of Forestry*,
volume 37, number 9, 1939, p. 727.

Leopold has been the most influential wilderness thinker since
Muir, and the Californian is indeed the authority most often cited in
A Sand County Almanac. But where Muir had been a pioneer plowman
himself, Leopold came from a more pedigreed background. Moreover,
by the time he grew up, America had become a technologically advanced and urbanized society. These differences in biography and
context might explain why Leopold's was an urbane, reflective approach, lacking the sheer *rawness* of Muir's engagement with nature.
John Muir, one might say, was a moralist and self-taught scientist,
Leopold a trained ecologist turned ethicist.

While Leopold and Muir both celebrated the wild, they are divided
in their attitude to what happened outside it. For Muir displayed in
abundance the siege-like mentality of the wilderness lover; he was
hostile to any force or form that might disturb the integrity of nature.
Thus his deep aversion to the 'marauding shepherds' who grazed their
flocks of 'hoofed locusts' in the national parks: these, along with
miners and timber contractors, were to him 'the Goths and vandals

of the wilderness, who are spreading black death in the fairest woods God ever made.' Muir thought the parks must be guarded by the military, for him the 'only effective and reliable arm of the government.' Soldiers with guns might make sure that 'not a single herd or cow be allowed to trample in the Yosemite garden,' a garden 'given to the State for a higher use than pasturage.'

In the view of Aldo Leopold, however, responsible human behavior *outside* the national parks was perhaps even more important than the protection of wild species within them. He urged private landowners to promote a mix of species on their holdings, thereby enhancing soil fertility and maintaining a diverse flora and fauna. Strict control of wild areas by the state mattered little unless individuals and communities moderated their consumption and respected nature. 'We need plants and birds and trees restored to ten thousand farms,' he wrote, 'not merely to a few paltry reservations.' As the Harvard historian Donald Fleming has remarked, for Leopold

> The virtue of small farms and rural living was the homely private transactions with nature to which they lent themselves, the untremendous and unpremeditated encounters knit into the fabric of daily life. National parks and national forests were seen as the goal of a pilgrimage, holy places set apart under the care of a jealous priesthood of conservationists, against the day when a lay believer, once in a lifetime, would conform to the faith in some cathedral-of-pines. This was the core of Leopold's objections to the Transcendentalists posture towards nature. It was irrevocably coupled to the idea of retreats from practical life, and worse still, to a corresponding devaluation of the workaday world as an appropriate arena for cherishing the natural environment. Leopold's own purpose was exactly the opposite. He wanted to strip the conservation ideal of its remote and sacred aspects and make the cultivation of a loving and wondering attitude toward other organisms and toward the land itself a matter of voluntary daily practice in modest contexts, particularly when men were unobserved and unintoxicated by the gigantic and patently sublime.

Aldo Leopold differed not only from John Muir but from dozens of wilderness thinkers before or since, who have had time only for spectacular habitats like the seas and the mountains, and for charismatic animals such as the tiger and the whale. These thinkers have focused narrowly, too narrowly perhaps, on the creation of parks and sanctuaries policed from within and protected by walls and fences from without. Leopold's was a more inclusive approach, and this in more than one respect. Ecologically, he moved from the protection of species to the protection of habitats and on toward the protection of all forms of biological diversity. Socially, he recognized that wild areas could hardly be saved without a wider reorganization of the economy on ecological principles, so that the fruits of nature's use could be more equitably distributed among humans. Ethically, he hoped that an attitude of care and wonder towards nature would not be expressed only on occasional excursions into the wild, but come to be part of the fabric of our daily lives, so that on weekdays, as much as on weekends, we would come to tread gently on this earth.

Some Who Don't Fit

Scientific conservation, back-to-the-land, and wilderness thinking have been the most influential ideologies of the first wave of environmentalism. Into one or other of these three modes would fit numerous thinkers and strands across the continents, by no means all of whom have been featured in this narrative. Rather than add to the list of representative thinkers, I shall in conclusion consider a trinity of environmentalists who cannot be easily slotted into any of these categories. Analytical rather than argumentative, reflective rather than passionate, this trio is remembered for helping build bridges between the natural sciences and the social sciences, as forerunners of the 'inter-disciplinary' and 'trans-disciplinary' intellectual movements of the present day.

The first of these unclassifiable environmentalists is the Scotsman Patrick Geddes (1854–1932), an admirer of John Ruskin and George Perkins Marsh but withal an original thinker in his own right. In a long and colorful career Geddes taught botany at Dundee and sociology in Bombay, ran a museum in Edinburgh and established a college in the south of France. 'By both training and general habit of mind,' wrote one of his students, Geddes was 'an ecologist long before that branch of biology had obtained the status of a special discipline.' However, Geddes was not so much a biological ecologist as a *social* ecologist, a scholar who sought to understand the dynamic inter-relationships between human societies and their natural environments.

Geddes' most significant work, in an intellectual as well as practical sense, was in the field of town and city planning. He was one of the first thinkers to highlight the parasitism of the modern city, its

Lewis Mumford & Patrick Geddes
THE CORRESPONDENCE

EDITED AND INTRODUCED BY
Frank G. Novak, Jr.

Book of correspondence between Patrick Geddes and Lewis Mumford, Scottish environmentalist and his Manhattan disciple.

SOURCE Frank G. Novack, Jr., Lewis Mumford and Patrick Geddes: The Correspondence *(Routledge)* exploitation of the rural hinterland through its voracious appetite for energy and materials. The dependence of the industrial city on fossil fuels, and the tremendous pollution this engendered, were captured in his evocative phrase, 'carboniferous capitalism.' Geddes wrote dozens of plans for cities in Europe and Asia, each of which aimed at harmonizing urban living with the values and virtues of the countryside. He thus called for 'a return to the health of village life, with its beauty of surroundings and its contact with nature,' but 'upon a new spiral turning beyond the old one, which, at the same time, frankly and fully incorporates the best advantages of town life.' Town planning, in his view, should aim above all at 'the Conservation of Nature and for the increase of our accesses to her.' His own plans—which, alas, were rarely followed or implemented—stressed the creation of open spaces and parks, the planting and protection of trees, and the conservation of water and water bodies.

Geddes' ideas were carried forward by two of his outstanding disciples, the American historian Lewis Mumford (1895–1986) and the Indian sociologist Radhakamal Mukherjee (1889–1966). Active as a writer and thinker for over fifty years, Mumford spanned the two waves of the environmental movement, and made notable contributions to both. Like Muir and Gandhi before him, Mumford did not have a college education: his own university, he liked to say, was the city of Manhattan, where he grew up and in whose streets and parks and libraries he learnt of life. He was to write insightfully on this and other cities, on the environment within them and on the region of which they formed part. Mumford's published works include a couple of dozen books and a couple of hundred essays, all of which owed as much to his own lived experience as to book learning.

Mumford argued that the organic unity between the city and the hinterland, characteristic of medieval Europe, had been disturbed by the coal-and-iron based industrialization of the nineteenth century, whose most distinctive features were the polluting factory and the unhygienic slum—indeed, it was 'plain that never before in recorded history had such vast masses of people lived in such a savagely deteriorated environment.' But Mumford looked forward, not backwards, hoping for the emergence of a new, post-industrial phase of economic development, based on non-polluting sources of energy, such as solar power and hydroelectricity, and on long-lasting alloys. The society he wished for would restore three disturbed equilibria: the equilibrium between the city and the village; the equilibrium in population, by balancing birth and death rates; and, most vital of all, the equilibrium between humans and nature.

As a historian, Mumford studied dispassionately the emergence of the 'money economy of destruction;' while as a citizen he worked actively for 'the future life economy of renewal.' The roles of scholar and activist were also combined in the person of Radhakamal Mukherjee, a sociologist who fell under Geddes' sway when the latter lived in India, between 1915 and 1922. Where other social scientists studied humans in isolation from nature, Mukherjee insisted that any social group must be considered in relation to 'the interwoven chain of biotic communities to which it is inextricably linked, the plants it cultivates, the animals it breeds, and even the insects which are indigenous to a region.' In the region that he most closely studied, the Indo-Gangetic plain, he found 'exhaustion and depletion' everywhere—in the form of deforestation, soil erosion, and declining yields—this in place of the 'renewal and enrichment of nature' which should legitimately be man's goal. He thus called for an 'alliance with the entire range of ecological forces' through the 'imparting of new values—the thought for tomorrow, the sacrifice for the inhabitants of the region yet unborn.'

Combining reason with passion, the Geddes-Mukherjee-Mumford tradition of social ecology goes beyond the partial visions of other traditions of environmentalism. Its key analytical category, 'the region,' brings together the three realms—of the wilderness, the countryside, and the city—which other schools tend to view in isolation. For a regionalist program works simultaneously for the preservation of the primeval wild, the restoration of a stable rural community, and for an urban-industrial complex that is sustainable without being parasitical. In 1938, Louis Mumford demarcated this approach from the mainstream environmental movement. Mumford wrote that

> originating in the spectacle of waste and defilement, the conservation movement has tended to have a negative influence : it has sought to isolate wilderness areas from encroachment and it has endeavoured to diminish waste and prevent damage. The present task of regional planning is a more positive one: it seeks to bring the earth as a whole up to the highest pitch of perfection and appropriate use—not merely preserving the primeval, but extending the range of the garden, and introducing the deliberate culture of the landscape into every part of the open country.

The next year the world was at war, and environmentalism in all its varieties was relegated to the margins of public life.

The Age of
Ecological Innocence

However appealing it might seem to some today, the 'green agenda' with which we ended Part I found few takers at the time. The reason for this was not its intrinsic weaknesses but rather its overshadowing by an event of truly global consequences, known appropriately as the Second *World* War. The human costs of the holocaust of 1939–45 were to exceed those of the battles of 1914–18, yet the outcome was very different. The First World War had cast a pall of gloom over the thinkers of Europe, a good many of whom sought imaginative refuge in a pre-industrial past when war between neighbors did not seem to exact such a terrible price. In contrast, the Allied victory in 1945 was to fuel a visible optimism with regard to the future of humanity.

Unlike its predecessor, World War II was more readily understood as a struggle of good against evil, the freedom-loving democracies of Britain and the U.S.A. versus the authoritarian and Fascist states of Italy and Germany. Moreover, the 'right' side won. No such clear-cut identification of virtue and vice was possible with respect to World War I, which was merely a conflict between rival imperialists over materials and territories. The moral salience of World War II was underscored when its end was quickly followed by the granting by Britain of independence in 1947 to the 'jewel in the crown' of its empire, India. The Western powers, it appeared, were affirming their commitment to democracy by getting rid of their colonial possessions. Other nations were to follow the British example, although political independence was in most countries an outcome as much of militant nationalism as of the benevolence of departing colonialists. The Dutch left Indonesia in 1948, the Americans gave up the Philippines the next year, while Britain progressively withdrew from its numerous colonies in Asia and Africa. Most reluctant to go home were the French and the Portuguese, who had to fight bitter and bloody wars—in Algeria and Indo-China in the one case, in Angola and Mozambique in the other—before finally conceding that the epoch of white rule over colored peoples had irrevocably passed.

The consequences of peace in Europe/America and decolonization in Asia/Africa were in one crucial respect the same. In both contexts, the supreme task of governments was now to fulfil, and if possible to exceed, the *economic* expectations of their citizens. In the North, intellectuals and politicians alike believed that the generation and distribution of wealth, more than anything else, would help wipe away the memories of war. For the victory achieved in the far-flung battlefields of the Second World War was widely perceived to be a victory for technology as much as for democracy. The conflict ended, the route to future salvation seemed to lie in the fruitful application of technology to the production process. As President Truman insisted in his inauguration speech of January 20, 1949, 'greater production is the key to prosperity and peace.'

The 'preoccupation with productivity and production' which the economist John Kenneth Galbraith was to see so manifest in post-War America was in fact quite characteristic of post-War Europe as well. The population in these societies had for the most part been adequately housed, clothed, and fed; now they expressed a desire for 'more elegant cars, more exotic food, more erotic clothing, more elaborate entertainment.' When Galbraith termed 1950s America the 'affluent society' he meant not only that this was a society most of whose members were hugely prosperous when reckoned against other societies and other times, but also that this was a society so dedicated to affluence that the possession and consumption of material goods became the exclusive standard of individual and collective achievement. This was a culture, remarked the anthropologist Geoffrey Gorer, in which 'any device or regulation which interfered, or can be conceived as interfering, with [the] supply of more and better things is resisted with unreasoning horror, as the religious resist blasphemy, or the warlike pacifism.' While addressing Congress in 1941, one of the greatest of American presidents, Franklin Roosevelt, had looked forward to a 'world founded upon four essential freedoms:' the freedom of expression and of worship, and the freedom from want and from fear. A decade later, with the war in a safe past, it seemed as if the four freedoms most cherished by society were the freedom to produce, to consume, to get get richer.

The newly independent nations of Asia and Africa we occupied with productivity and production, but with the removal of poverty rather than the generation of greater affluence as their goal— this corresponding to the third of Roosevelt's original list, the 'freedom from want everywhere in the world.' Nationalists like Nehru in India, Sukarno in Indonesia, and Nasser in Egypt were united by the belief that imperialism had only been made possible by the economic and technological superiority of the colonial powers. Decolonization had opened up the possibility of these previously 'underdeveloped' nations 'developing' along the same lines as the West. Rapid industrialization, it was thought, would end poverty and unemployment and make for a strong and self-reliant society.

Now, when there is so much cynicism abroad about the very idea of 'development', it is good to remember the deeply humane and democratic sensibilities that underlay its original formulation. The age of empire had been governed by the belief that white was superior to brown and black, but the idea of development implied that people *everywhere* had equal rights and capabilities. Inequalities between or within nations were not natural or pre-ordained; rather, they could be removed (or at least mitigated) by concerted social action. Modern science and technology, theoretically within reach of all, provided one plank of this equalizing effort; the other was the new nation-state, often headed by a charismatic leader embodying the hopes and aspirations of millions of ordinary people. In India, for example, the state, as well as the process of economic development itself, was ruled over by a Prime Minister (Nehru) whose personal popularity surpassed that of Mahatma Gandhi at the height of his fame; while behind him stood a Congress party which had led a multi-class freedom movement and since come to power through the ballot box rather than the bullet.

The sincerity and legitimacy of the 'developers' duly noted, one must nonetheless recognize that the times were scarcely propitious for the formulation or advancement of an environmentalist agenda. With the overwhelming focus on production, environmentally oriented thinking—in the domains of the city, countryside, or forest— could find little play. For opinion-makers in the 'affluent society' and in the 'developing country' likewise called for a more intensive use of nature and natural resources. The twenty years after World

War II are known as the 'development decades,' but they might more accurately be termed the 'age of ecological innocence.' In the U.S. as much as in India, in Britain as well as in Brazil, talk of ecological constraints to economic growth was regarded as irrelevant at best, and at worst as a dangerous deviation from the primary national task, defined in one context as the generation of affluence and in the other as the lessening of the gap between rich and poor nations. The air was suffused with optimism; especially the optimism of the technologist. Characteristic here are some remarks of the U.S. secretary of the treasury, Henry Morgenthau, offered at the founding of the International Bank for Reconstruction and Development (the World Bank) in 1945. The Bank, wrote Morgenthau confidently, would help create 'a dynamic world economy in which the peoples of every nation will be able to enjoy, increasingly, the fruits of material progress on an earth *infinitely* blessed with natural riches.'

In this manner, the prospect of unending economic growth was held out to the people of the North, the prospect of becoming exactly like America, and living like Americans, offered to the underdeveloped world. Science was said to be the 'endless frontier,' technology the 'inexhaustible resource;' working in harness, they would dispel any thoughts of resource shortages, temporary or permanent. Such was the view of the men who both defined and deified the age of ecological innocence, for instance Vannevar Bush of NASA or the geologist Kirtley F. Mather of Harvard University, who believed that Mother Earth herself had 'enough and to spare.'

To be sure, there was the odd discordant voice. One was the great Berkeley geographer Carl Sauer, who located the current of buoyant optimism firmly in time and place. He remarked that 'the doctrine of a passing frontier of nature replaced by a permanent and sufficiently expanding frontier of technology is a contemporary and characteristic expression of occidental culture, itself a historical-geographical product.' This frontier attitude, he went on, 'has the recklessness of an optimism that has become habitual, but which is residual from the brave days when north-European freebooters overran the world and put it under tribute.' Warning that the surge of growth at the expense of nature would not last indefinitely, Sauer—speaking for his fellow Occidentals—noted wistfully that 'we have not yet learned the difference between yield and loot. We do not like to be economic realists.'

A second dissident was E. F. Schumacher, a German economist who had fled Nazism to settle in England. Schumacher believed that

the 'economic expansion [which] is the common ideology of all mankind today' had legitimized the rapacious exploitation of non-renew-
able resources such as coal and oil. 'We forget that we are living off
capital in the most fundamental meaning of the word,' he wrote in
1954, adding: 'Mankind has existed for many thousands of years and
has always lived off income. Only in the last hundred years has man
forcibly broken into nature's larder and is now emptying it out at a
breathtaking speed which increases from year to year.' Yet another
prescient voice was Lewis Mumford, who was more concerned with
the instruments by which nature was being ravaged. Writing in 1955,
he warned that the 'awful omniscience and the omnipotence of our
science and technology' might 'turn out to be more self-destructive
than ignorance and impotence.' He deplored the rule of 'power, prestige and profit,' insisting that 'only when love takes the lead will the
earth, and life on earth, be safe again.'

Sauer, Schumacher and Mumford are all recognizably part of the
history of Western environmentalism. Let us now consider a dissenter
unknown to that history. Mira Behn—her real name was Madeleine
Slade—was the daughter of an English admiral who joined Mahatma
Gandhi in 1927 and spent the next thirty years in the service of her
teacher and his land. Shortly after the war she moved from Gandhi's
ashram in central India to a village in the Himalaya, seeking to understand the rhythms of nature and the relation of peasant life to it. Her
primary concern, as befitting a Gandhian, was with the rehabilitation
of the village economy, but at times, as befitting an Englishwoman,
she expressed an almost Wordsworthian affinity with nature. Herself
a 'devotee of the great primeval Mother Earth,' she complained in
April 1949 that

> The tragedy today is that educated and moneyed classes are altogether
> out of touch with the vital fundamentals of existence—our Mother
> Earth, and the animal and vegetable population which she sustains. This
> world of Nature's planning is ruthlessly plundered, despoiled and dis-
> organized by man whenever he gets the chance. By his science and
> machinery he may get huge returns for a time, but ultimately will come
> desolation. We have got to study Nature's balance, and develop our lives
> within her laws, if we are to survive as a physically healthy and morally
> decent species.

As it happens, Mira Behn could hardly have been less in tune with
the society in which she lived, and in later life she settled near Vienna
to seek out the spirit of Beethoven—yet another dedicated German

nature-lover. Meanwhile independent India was restless, on the move, determined to conquer and master nature rather than submit silently to its laws. This called for the construction of steel mills and atomic power plants, not the organic farms and village woodlots which the Gandhians advocated. Likewise, Lewis Mumford's regionalist program, which had found ready adherents in the 1930s, had no place in an America that now took the globe as its oyster. E. F. Schumacher was also to battle unsuccessfully against 'a vision of a future when technology would ensure that there was plenty for all'—as his biographer tells us, 'no one was [then] interested in listening to an economist who told them that [their] future was built on dreams.' Incomprehension, indifference and hostility were what faced those who dared challenge the age of ecological innocence, a phase which stretched from the end of the Second World War to the last quarter of 1962. It was in that year that the second wave of environmentalism announced itself through the unlikely medium of a newly published book.

5

The Ecology of Affluence

THE SIGNIFICANCE OF
SILENT SPRING

Put two historians in a room and you have a debate; put a couple more and you have a cacophony of discordant voices. In a tribe notorious for disputation and disagreement, there is a surprising unanimity on what begat modern environmentalism. 'The landmark book *Silent Spring*,' writes Ralph H. Lutts, 'played a vitally important role in stimulating the contemporary environmental movement.' Stephen Fox goes further: *Silent Spring*, he says, 'became one of the seminal volumes in conservation history: the *Uncle Tom's Cabin* of modern environmentalism.' Kirkpatrick Sale is more categorical still; he quotes a stirring paragraph from the preface of the book in question, and adds: 'With those angry and uncompromising words, it can be said that the modern environmental movement began.'

Silent Spring was the work of Rachel Carson, a biologist who had worked for years with the U.S. Fish and Wildlife Service, and was the author previously of two best-selling but non-controversial books on the sea. The influence of her third book might be judged by numbers: by the fact that *Silent Spring* sold half-a-million copies in hard cover, the fact that it stayed thirty-one weeks on the *New York Times* bestseller list, the fact that it was quickly published, in English or in translation, in some two dozen countries. The book's impact is also measured, in the historians' accounts, by the controversies it generated in the media, in corporate boardrooms, in scientific journals and within government departments.

The curious thing, however, is that *Silent Spring* is apparently not much read any more. Historians of the environmental movement have dwelt at length on its impact, a few among them have offered potted biographies of the author, yet one is hard put to find in the published literature an intelligent summary and assessment of the book itself. And that is a pity, for *Silent Spring* is a truly remarkable work, a contribution to science that is worth reading—and re-reading—for its literary qualities alone.

For Rachel Carson the 'central problem of our age' was the 'contamination of man's total environment with substances of incredible potential for harm.' These were the new chemicals patented during and after the war, such as dicholoro-diphenyl-trichloroethane (DDT), an insecticide that had found wide favor among farmers and scientists. DDT was only the most prominent of an array of pesticides synthesized by chemists for use on the farm and in the factory. Between 1947 and 1960, the output of pesticides in the U.S. jumped from 1.24 to 6.37 million pounds; moreover 'in the plans and hopes of the industry this enormous production [was] only a beginning.' Used for a worthy purpose—to increase food production by eliminating pests—these manipulated chemicals had become, in Carson's colorful language, 'elixirs of death,' a 'battery of poisons of truly extraordinary powers.' As she explained, chemicals applied to plants and trees slowly leached into the soil and water, thereupon entering the food chain. Passing from one organism to another, from insects and birds to fish and animals, they went on to enter the bodies of humans in repeated small doses. These chemicals, modeled in the laboratory with little regard to their impact on the natural world, thus constituted an ever-present if insidiously invisible danger to diverse forms of life.

The early chapters of *Silent Spring* describe these new chemicals, their applications and impact on soil, water, and forests. The book then moves on to a defense of nature against these modern and, in the author's view, unwarranted intrusions. A chapter on wildlife is followed by one on birds, centered on deaths of robins in parts of New England, poisoned by eating worms contaminated by insecticides sprayed on the elm tree—a perfect example of how the poisons worked their way up the food chain. It was this threat to a loved and familiar bird that the book's title evoked: 'the sudden silencing of the song of birds, the obliteration of the color and beauty and interest they lent to our world,' such that 'spring now comes unheralded' by their return, with 'the early mornings strangely silent where once they were filled with the beauty of bird song.' This was certainly the reality in a few villages and towns here and there, but the work's power lay in its suggestion that this could become the norm *throughout* North America, unless humans worked quickly to control pesticides.

Only a little less loved than the robin was the eagle, America's national bird, and the salmon, that sprightly fish so lovingly memorialized in poetry and myth. Carson provides accounts of eagle kills and salmon deaths, before arriving finally at the threat to human life through chemical ingestion, most dramatically illustrated by the increasing incidence of cancer. Here too the narrative is full of foreboding—Carson herself was diagnosed as suffering from cancer while working on *Silent Spring*—but the book ends with an offering of hope, the hope that biological methods of pest control would give humans a last chance to 'reach a destination that assures the preservation of our earth.' Biological methods had been tested in other countries; Carson quotes the distinguished Dutch entomologist C. J. Brejér in support of her own view that scientists had to commence

> some very energetic research on other control measures, measures that will have to be biological, not chemical. Our aim should be to guide natural processes as cautiously as possible in the desired direction rather than to use brute force . . . Life is a miracle beyond our comprehension, and we should reverence it even when we have to struggle against it. . . . Humbleness is in order; there is no excuse for scientific conceit here.

Silent Spring is a marvel of popular and partisan science, rich in well chosen examples and carefully detailed case studies drawn from specialized scientific works, here arranged and presented to the public in beautifully crafted prose. Beneath and beyond the facts lay a deeper philosophical argument, to the effect that nature was to be respected as a 'complex, precise and highly integrated system of relationships between living things which cannot safely be ignored any more than the law of gravity can be defied with impunity by a man perched on the edge of a cliff.'

Environmentalists had for some time been concerned with the protection of endangered species or beautiful habitats; it was *Silent Spring* which helped them move further, to an appreciation that 'in nature nothing exists alone,' that 'there are intimate and essential relations between plants and the earth, between plants and other plants, between plants and animals:' that nature was, in sum, 'an intricate web of life whose interwoven strands lead from microbes to man.' The interconnectedness of all life called for a modest, gentle and cautious attitude toward nature, rather than the arrogant, aggressive and intrepid route taken by synthetic chemistry and its products. Otherwise the web of life could very easily become the web of death.

Silent Spring's impact was not, of course, contingent on an acceptance of this philosophy of nature, for the facts of pesticide abuse and its consequences for wildlife and humans spoke for themselves. The book, noted a historian twenty years after its publication, found a constituency broader 'than that enjoyed by any previous environmental issue. Never before had so diverse a body of people, from bird watchers, to wildlife managers and public health professionals, to suburban homeowners, been joined together to deal with a [common] threat.' Early admirers of *Silent Spring* included the secretary of the interior, Stewart Udall, and President John F. Kennedy himself, whose Scientific Advisory Committee put out a report endorsing Carson's conclusions.

The consequences of the book were far-reaching. In the wake of *Silent Spring* towns 'reconsidered their foolish herbicidal assaults' on avenue shrubs and trees; citizens and officials became more alert to potential fish kills in rivers; senators and congressmen were energized to make pesticide production a subject for political debate and legislative enactment; a federal committe on pest control was established to scrutinize new products; the U.S. department of agriculture, once a keen enthusiast for synthetic pesticides, outlawed several dangerous chemicals; dozens of states and the Federal Government outlawed the use of the most deadly of them all, DDT; and finally, a Pesticide Control Act of 1972 and a Toxic Substances Control Act of 1974 gave legal teeth to attempts to more closely control and monitor chemicals. Not since the appearance of John Maynard Keynes' *General Theory of Employment, Interest and Money*—which was published in England in 1937—did a single book have such a dramatic and simultaneous impact on public opinion, scientific research, and state policy.

The impact of *Silent Spring* was by no means restricted to the United States. Carson herself acknowledged foreign influences on her work; on the scientific side, the Dutch entomologist C. J. Brejér provided some key arguments, while the concept of 'food chain,' used in the book to such telling effect, had first been elaborated by the great Oxford ecologist Charles Elton, an authority several times quoted respectfully by the author. The book was dedicated to the Alsatian doctor Albert Schweitzer, begetter of the philosophy of 'reverence for life,' while its epigraph came from the English poet John Keats: 'The sedge is wither'd from the lake, And no birds sing'— words which provided the book with its title and its most effective image.

Rachel Carson was no narrow nationalist, yet her debts to other cultures were to be duly returned, with interest. Translated into twelve languages, *Silent Spring* had a striking impact on the resurgence of environmentalism throughout Europe. A historian of Germany explains how in that country 'the translation of [this] landmark polemic stood as a best-seller for many months,' its 'echo seen in the sharp upsurge' of membership of conservation organizations. A sociologist of Sweden writes that in his country 'it was Carson's book that served to usher in the modern era of environmentalism.' In Britain, the publication of the book provoked a furious debate in the House of Lords; outside that august body, it came to the attention of the biologist Julian Huxley. Through reading *Silent Spring* Huxley realized that in Britian too the new insecticides and herbicides were decimating plant and animal life; when he communicated this to his brother Aldous, the famous writer remarked that 'we are losing half the subject-matter of English poetry,' a comment that—had it reached her—would have greatly pleased Carson.

In the American context, *Silent Spring* is best compared to George Perkins Marsh's monumental *Man and Nature*, likewise a model of scientific clarity and exhaustiveness, and likewise a call to action aimed at scientists as well as to the public at large. It is unlikely that Rachel Carson herself thought of this comparison. For the author of *Silent Spring* wrote as if unaware of the first wave of environmentalism, as if there did not exist an authentically American tradition of respect and reverence for the integrity of nature. John Muir admired George Perkins Marsh, Aldo Leopold honored Muir, but Carson does not mention any of the great trio that preceded her. Her book did not go back beyond the Second World War, the event which set in motion the production and dissemination of the chemicals which were her immediate concern. This focus was understandable, but it is notable nonetheless that she fails to acknowledge that her nature philosophy had such a distinguished pedigree. Her silence in this regard is testimony perhaps to the hold of the Age of Ecological Innocence, which seems to have so effectively wiped away the memory and heritage of the first wave of environmentalism.

WAVES WITHIN THE WAVE

The Environmental Debate

Early in her book, Rachel Carson identified two reasons for the lack of awareness with regard to the new chemicals. 'This is an era of specialists,' she explained, 'each of whom sees his own problem and is unaware of or intolerant of the larger frame into which it fits. It is also an era dominated by industry, in which the right to make a dollar at whatever cost is seldom challenged.'

Carson herself was more concerned with the specialists, her book an extended polemic against narrow-minded chemists by one who was obliged on account of her own training to be always mindful of the 'larger frame.' Chemical controls, she wrote, 'have been devised and applied without taking into account the complex biological systems against which they have been blindly hurled.' Her remarks are laced with sarcasm—e.g., 'the chemists' ingenuity in devising insecticides has long ago outrun biological knowledge of the way these poisons affect the living organism'—and her book ends with an utter condemnation of the science of specialists:

> The concepts and practices of applied entomology for the most part date from the Stone Age of science. It is our alarming misfortune that so primitive a science has armed [itself] with the most modern and terrible weapons, and that in turning them against the insects it has also turned them against the earth.

This theme was underlined by Julian Huxley in his foreword to the British edition of *Silent Spring*. Pest control, he wrote, 'is of course necessary and desirable, but it is an ecological matter, and cannot be handed over entirely to the chemists.' Like Carson, Huxley was a biologist, schooled in a science that in three major respects differs from the disciplines of physics and chemistry. First, biologists are taught to look for interdependence in nature, viewing individual life forms not in isolation but in relation to one another. Ever since Darwin, biologists have also been oriented toward a longer time frame, thinking in aeons and generations rather than months and years. Finally, biologists have a direct professional interest in species other than humans; as ornithologists, botanists and zoologists, they are, willy-nilly, more alert to the interests of bird, plant or animal life.

Inspired by Carson, though sometimes following lines tangential to hers, other biologists also came to play a disproportionate role in shaping the environmental debate of the sixties and seventies. Environmental 'classics' that appeared in the decade following *Silent*

Spring include Raymond Dasmann's evocation of the threatened beauty of a great American state; Paul Ehrlich's grim prediction of collective human suicide through over-breeding; Garret Hardin's equally despairing parable of how human society would self-destruct through aggressive competition over nature and natural resources; and Barry Commoner's urbane extension of Carson's attack on one-eyed science, where atomic physics was placed alongside synthetic chemistry. All these works were written by biologists, and all had apocalyptic titles: *The Destruction of California* (Dasmann); *The Population Bomb* (Ehrlich); *The Tragedy of the Commons* (Hardin); *The Closing Circle* (Commoner).

These works were closely followed in Europe, but in that continent too home-grown biologists were to emerge as major spokesmen for the new environmentalism. In Sweden the microbiologist Bjorn Gillberg and the biochemist Hans Palmstierma came to prominence in the late sixties as authors of scholary studies on chemical hazards as well as of numerous popular articles in the press. Their counterpart in the Netherlands was C. J. Brejér, a friend of Carson who in 1967 produced his own influential version of *Silent Spring* entitled *Zilveren Sluiersen Verborgen Sevaren* (Silver Veils and Hidden Dangers). Among the first to ring the alarm bells in the United Kingdom were Eric Ashby, F. Fraser Darling, C. H. Waddington and Julian Huxley, all eminent biologists with a more than professional interest in protecting the environment.

This is not to say that only biologists contributed to the burgeoning literature and intensifying public debate. E. F. Schumacher, still a dissident among economists, found his moment had arrived in 1973 when he published *Small is Beautiful*, a book much admired for its espousal of a 'Buddhist' economics based on 'appropriate' technology—that is, machines and production processes that would be cheap, decentralized, use little energy, and be sensitive to the environment. Schumacher had been deeply influenced by Gandhi, and by a trip he made to India in the early sixties (see *box*). Important contributions also came from the California historian Lynn White Jr. and the Norwegian philosopher Arné Naess, both concerned with the ethical and religious aspects of our relations with nature. More influential than these single-authored works was the collaborative *Limits to Growth*, a study commissioned by the Club of Rome which argued on the basis of computer simulations that current trends in population growth, energy demand and resource consumption were pressing hard on the carrying capacity of the earth. Published in 1972, *Limits* appeared in thirty languages and sold some four million copies in all.

One man who saw his life's work vindicated by the new environmental consciousness was Lewis Mumford. Born in 1895, Mumford had lived long enough to influence the first wave of environmentalism, to welcome the second, and, not least, to protest vigorously against the age of innocence which came in between. In October 1962, weeks after Rachel Carson's book appeared, Mumford was due to speak at the Davis campus of the University of California. Although I have no conclusive proof, he must already have read *Silent Spring*—if not the whole book, at least the extracts that had appeared previously in the *New Yorker* (a magazine he too wrote for). In any

---

ECONOMICS AS WISDOM

The German-British scholar E. F. Schumacher explains what he means by an 'economics of permanence;' he invokes Gandhi, but not his follower J. C. Kumarappa, who back in 1945 had written a book with a tantalizingly similar title, 'The Economy of Permanence.'

From an economic point of view, the central concept of Wisdom is Permanence. We must study the Economics of Permanence. Nothing makes economic sense unless its continuance for a long time can be projected without running into absurdities. There can be 'growth' towards a limited objective, but there cannot be unlimited, generalized growth. It is likely, as Gandhi said, that 'Earth provides enough to satisfy every man's need, but not for every man's greed.' Permanence is incompatible with a predatory attitude which rejoices in the fact that 'what were luxuries for our fathers have become necessities for us.'

. . . The Economics of Permanence implies a profound re-orientation of science and technology, which have to open their doors to Wisdom . . . Scientific or technological 'solutions' which poison the environment or degrade the social structure and man himself, are of no benefit, no matter how brilliantly conceived or how great their superficial attraction. Ever bigger machines, entailing ever bigger concentrations of economic power and exerting ever greater violence against the environment do not represent progress: they are a denial of Wisdom. Wisdom demands a new orientation of science and technology towards the organic, the gentle, the non-violent, the elegant and beautiful. . . . We must look for a revolution in technology to give us inventions and machines which reverse the destructive trends now threatening us all.

Source: E. F. Schumacher, 'The economics of permanence,' *Resurgence*, volume 3, number 1, May/June 1970, reprinted in Robin Clarke, editor, *Notes for the Future: An Alternative History of the Past Decade* (London: Thames and Hudson, 1975).

event, his message was entirely consistent with Carson's. Mumford first outlined the history of ecological abuse on the American continent, beginning with the pioneers and culminating in the polluting epoch of what he, following Patrick Geddes, liked to call 'carboniferous capitalism.' He asked his student audience to replace the reigning myth of the machine with 'a new myth of life, a myth based upon a richer understanding of all organic processes,' a myth that would help humans work 'in co-operative relation with all the forces of nature.' Three years later, addressing a conference of ecologists, he urged scientists to place their particular concerns in a broader frame. 'When we rally to preserve the remaining redwood forests or to protect the whooping crane,' he said, 'we are rallying to preserve ourselves, we are trying to keep in existence the organic variety, the whole span of natural resources, upon which our own further development will be based.'

The historian Donald Fleming once remarked that the resurgence of environmentalism in the sixties allowed Mumford to 'reconstruct and amplify the themes of a lifetime.' The themes were the same, but a new urgency had now manifested itself in the sage's pronouncements. As he wrote in 1973, 'the chief effect of the regressive transformations that have taken place in the last quarter of a century [i.e. since the end of World War II] has been to change my conclusions from the indicative to the imperative mood; not "we shall" achieve a dynamic equilibrium [between humans and nature] but *"we must"*— if we are not to destroy the ecological balance upon which all life depends.'

In both Europe and North America, then, there was a prolific outcrop of environmentalist tracts in the years following the appearance of *Silent Spring*. Some of these works were sober and scholarly, others passionate and polemical. Several carried forward traditions characteristic of the movement's first wave. Thus the heritage of wilderness thinking was manifest in 'Neo-Malthusians' such as Garret Hardin and Paul Ehrlich, who worried that exploding human populations were dangerously encroaching on the living space of other species. It was also manifest in the ideas-centered work of Arné Naess and Lynn White, who like Muir and Leopold before them complained that most of their fellow humans sought to tame and dominate nature rather than understand or cherish her. Likewise, the traditions of scientific conservation were reinvigorated by the technocrats—as for instance the members of the Club of Rome—who sought to moderate world economic development toward a sustainable path, and by the more radical 'eco-socialists,' like Barry Commoner, who

called for alternate, non-polluting technologies and welcomed greater
state control over the processes of production. Least visible of the
older trends was 'Back-to-the-Land,' for by the 1960s peasants were
no longer around in most of Europe to be defended or identified
with. Yet the voices of Ruskin and Carpenter do resonate with Schumacher's *Small is Beautiful*, and with the *Blueprint for Survival*, issued in 1972 by the London-based *Ecologist* magazine: both works
that not so much defended nature as mounted a wholesale attack on
the excesses of industrial civilization. 'The principal defect of the industrial way of life,' announced the authors of *Blueprint*, 'is that it is
not sustainable. Its termination within the lifetime of someone born
today is inevitable—unless it continues to be sustained for a while
longer by an entrenched minority at the cost of imposing great suffering on the rest of mankind.'

These modern manifestations of older traditions disagreed bitterly amongst themselves, but they are to be collectively distinguished
from their common enemy, the ruling ideology of the age of innocence. Thinkers of the latter persuasion turned on environmentalists
of all stripes, calling them 'backward-looking reactionaries,' 'prophets of doom,' and worse. It was not unknown for an environmentalist to be termed a CIA plant behind the Iron Curtain and a KGB
agent in the free world. Socialists accused greens of deviating attention from the class struggle, capitalists accused them of seeking to
impede the working of the market. The counterattack was led by
economists who believed that the market and technology would find
substitutes for any resource that went short or for rivers that ran dry.
Paul Samuelson of the Massachussets Institute of Technology, a future Nobel Prize winner, reacted sharply to the Club of Rome report, insisting that the 'wonders of the Industrial Revolution are not
over.' Across the Atlantic, Wilfrid Beckerman of London University
went so far as to predict that 'economic growth will continue un-
interrupted for 2,500 years.'

Economists measure growth by aggregate statistical measures such
as Gross National Product or Per Capita Income—numbers that often conceal a multitude of sins. Ecologists are more keenly interested in the components of growth, i.e. the technologies that produce
goods, the processes by which these goods are consumed, the cumul-
ative impact of production and consumption on the living systems
of the earth. Their orientation made them less sanguine: where economists looked buoyantly forward to increases in GNP over the next
thousand years, ecologists looked back critically at what had happened in the last twenty-five. And wherever they looked they saw or

smelt danger, caused by the effluents of the dangerously novel technologies elaborated in the epoch of innocence. One such ecologist, Barry
Commoner, wrote unambiguously that—

> It is economic motivation that has impelled the sweeping anti-ecological
> changes in the technology of production that have occurred since the
> Second World War. These changes have turned the nation's factories,
> farms, vehicles, and shops into seed-beds of pollution: nitrates from
> fertilizer; phosphates from detergents; toxic residues from pesticides;
> smog and carcinogenic exhaust from vehicles; the growing list of toxic
> chemicals and the mounds of undegradable plastic containers, wrappings,
> and geegaws from the petrochemical industry.

Here were listed some of the *effluents of affluence*, to use a term coined
by the Spanish scholar Juan Martinez Alier. These effluents inspired
the work of scientists such as Carson and Commoner, but they were
also to generate a wider social response, an environmental *movement*
in addition to an environmental *debate*.

THE ENVIRONMENTAL MOVEMENT:
FROM IDEAS TO ACTIVISM

The University of Copenhagen, March 1969: a seminar on natural
history is in progress, with some of Denmark's foremost scientists in
attendance. A group of students enter the conference hall, lock the
doors, and cut off the ventilation. Shouting slogans against pollution, they burn garbage they have brought with them, spray water
from a polluted lake all over the participants, and hold aloft a duck
doused with oil. 'Come and save it,' they scream at the scientists:
'You talk about pollution, why don't you do anything about it.' An
hour of this hectoring and eerie symbolism elapses before the youths
open the doors. But their protest is not finished: they drag the naturalists off to the next room. In this room was being held the founding
meeting of NOAH, a body that would take Danish conservation
beyond genteel discussion toward systematic social action.

This dramatic episode captures the distance between environmentalism's first wave and its second. Muir and Leopold, Marsh and
Ruskin, were all 'activists' in their own way, yet their activism con-
sisted for the most part in speaking and writing, in using the power
of their words and the precision of their analyses to persuade others to join or follow them. Other conservationists worked closely with politicians and public officials, seeking to influence state
policies toward forest protection or water management. Contemporary environmentalism has by no means eschewed these strategies

of propaganda and advocacy, yet its potential has been greatly increased by its resort to more militant forms of action.

In this respect, of course, environmentalism has resembled other social movements of the late '60s and '70s. That was a time when the North Atlantic world was hit by a flurry of citizens' initiatives, exemplifying a new and participatory approach to politics. Willing on this process were several social movements that were to acquire distinct identities of their own: the feminist movement, the peace movement, the civil rights movement, and the environmental movement.

Environmentalism shared some tactics of protest with these other movements, but it was also to forge innovative methods of its own. Marches and processions in defense of the wild or in opposition to pollution were influenced by the civil rights struggle. The 'teach-in,' used to such good effect by the anti-war movement, was the model for a nation-wide effort, Earth Day, held on April 22, 1970, and described as 'the largest organized demonstration in human history.' In thousands of cities and towns spread across America, an estimated 20 million participants affirmed their commitment to a clean environment by planting trees, clearing up garbage, or silently protesting with placards outside polluting industries. Before and after Earth Day have occurred hundreds of more localized protests against more focused targets. Faced with a noxious chemical plant or an illegal toxic waste dump, with the coming in of chainsaws into their favorite forest or a dam being built on their favorite river, environmentalists took to the streets and increasingly to the courts to obtain redress. To 'Plant more Trees,' and 'Save the Grizzly' was added a more threatening slogan: 'Sue the Bastards.'

The Swedish sociologist Andrew Jamison has written of the new social movements that they were primarily the work of 'young people impatient with the political methods of their elders;' they represented, in effect, a 'revolt of the young.' With feminism and the peace movement, environmentalism was also driven by the energy and idealism of men and women in their twenties and thirties. But it did enjoy one clear advantage over the other movements: it was less divisive. Feminists would be accused of breaking up homes, civil rights workers of dividing black from white, peaceniks of ignoring the vital security interests of the nation. But in the U.S. at least, hundreds of thousands of citizens who suspiciously stayed away from those movements readily flocked to the green banner. When, after Earth Day 1970, the newsmagazine *Time* put Barry Commoner on its cover, it called him the 'Professor with a Class of Millions.' The mood of the times enabled scientists like Commoner and Ehrlich to command an audience far greater than that of the university classroom. This wider support for environmenal concerns could lend itself to a cynical inter-pretation. Environmentalism, suggests the sociologist Denton E. Mor-rison, 'came as something of a relief to a movement-pummeled white, middle-class America and its representatives in the power structure. The environmental movement especially seemed to have potential for diverting the energies of a substantial proportion of young people away from more bothersome movements and into [groups] that seemed to stand for something close to Country, God, Motherhood and Apple Pie, and that, at worst, [was] clearly the safest movement in town.'

It is unquestionably true that of the 'new' social movements en-vironmentalism alone has grown steadily in support and influence. Table I captures elements of this growth in statistical terms; it men-tions but four conservation groups, but there are numerous others which have grown in membership strength in these past decades. An estimated 14 million Americans, or one in every seven adults, are members of one or other environmental organization. Likewise, in both Britain and Germany some 5 million people are now involved as citizens in environmental pressure groups. And in the Nether-lands the foremost nature protection forum, the Vereniging tot Be-houd van Natuurmonumented, has increased its membership from 235,000 to 700,000 between 1980 and 1992.

Table I

Membership of selected U.S. conservation organizations
(in thousands)

Organization	Year				
	1966	*1970*	*1980*	*1985*	*1991*
Sierra Club	39	113	165	350	650
Audobon Society	41*	120	400	450	600
Wilderness Society	27**	54	50	100	350
National Wildlife Federation	272	540	818	825	5600

* figure for 1962   ** figure for 1964

Sources: Stephen Fox, *The American Conservation Movement: John Muir and His Legacy* (1985); Kirkpatrick Sale, *Green Revolutions: the American Environmental Movement, 1962–92* (1993).

This impressively large constituency can hardly be explained by the theory that environmentalism represents a 'safety valve' to defuse more threatening forms of collective action. Rather, the expansion of the mass base of the environmental movement is more plausibly related to corresponding changes in economy and society. For as the affluent society grew more affluent still, its members yearned for more arresting goods to consume. By the mid-sixties, cars, refrigerators and washing-machines had become commonplace, but holidays in the wild were not. The shift to a five-day week meant that consumers had both money and the means to travel. They now wished to escape, if only for a weekend or two, from their everyday milleu of factory or farm, city or suburb. Nature, whether in the form of forests to walk through, beaches to swim from, or mountains to climb and recline upon, provided the perfect—since temporary—antidote to industrial civilization. In 1964 a German magazine captured these manifold attractions of nature to the city-dweller:

> Here in Nature's reposed and silent forest, where there are no rows of houses, no noise of motors, no advertising lights, no machines and bank books, here, where the day-in, day-out, nerve-deranging concatenation of all doing with money . . . lies far behind us, the deepest essence of man, his soul and his spirit steps into its own. This value is not to be measured by money, and moreover [it] is granted free, without price and service charge.

> [translated from the German by Raymond H. Dominick III]

This message had a captive audience; between 1957 and 1972 the proportion of Germans who took vacation trips of a week or more rose from 36 per cent to 53 per cent. Nor was Germany exceptional; in Sweden, the increase in free time meant that 'more Swedes wanted to hunt, fish, bird-watch and collect berries, mushrooms and wild flowers in the forest.' In a nation of only 8.5 million people, as many as 600,000 came to own country cottages. In their working life these Swedes were caught up in 'the landscape of industrial production,' ruled by 'rationality, calculation, profit and effectiveness,' escaping on holidays and weekends to 'another landscape of recreation, contemplation, and romance.' All over the industrial world, as the historian Samuel Hays points out, 'natural environments which formerly had been looked upon as "useless" waiting only to be developed, now came to be thought of as "useful" for filling human wants and needs. They played no less a significant role in the advanced consumer society than did such material goods as hi fi sets or indoor gardens.'

This last quote seems to point to an uncomfortable gap between the environmental debate and the environmental movement. Scientists and ideologues were concerned with resource shortages and the disappearance of species. They were critical of the direction of economic growth and its impact on local, national or global ecosystems. Set against these prophets of doom was the growing popular interest in the wild and the beautiful, which not merely accepted the parameters of the affluent society but was wont to see nature itself as merely one more good to be 'consumed.' The uncertain commitment of most nature lovers to a more comprehensive environmental ideology is illustrated by the paradox that they were willing to drive thousands of miles, using up scarce oil and polluting the atmosphere, to visit national parks and sanctuaries; thus using anti-ecological means to marvel in the beauty of forests, swamps or mountains protected as specimens of a 'pristine' and 'untouched' nature.

The environmental groups fussed little about this gap betwen the prophets and the people. They were glad enough with the massive surge in their membership, which gave them the finances and legitimacy to push for legislative and political change. In the '70s and '80s these groups moved from activism in the streets and courts toward a more accommodating incorporation in the structures of governance. Environmentalists began to rely heavily on the expertise of scientists and lawyers who could work with rather than work against industry and government. As legislation was drafted for protecting nature or controlling the effluents of affluence, these specialists collaborated with state officials in fixing the permissible standards for industrial emissions, and identified particular species and habitats for designation as 'protected' or 'endangered.' In preparing briefs for legislators and sending forth emissaries to sit on scientific committees, the environmental movement helped set up and (in time) staff government departments, most notably the Environmental Protection Agency, which with 18,000 employees is currently the largest civilian arm of the U.S. government.

The routinization and professionalization of the environmental movement has in recent years generated a counter-movement, a struggle to return environmentalism to its confrontational past. In the U.S. this radical reaction has been led by the group Earth First! The group's founder, Dave Foreman, remarked some years ago that 'too many environmentalists have grown to resemble bureaucrats—pale from too much indoor light; weak from sitting too long behind desks; co-opted by too many politicians.' Warning his colleagues against 'playing the games of political compromise the industrial power-brokers have designed for us,' Foreman thought the 'time has come to translate the non-violent methods of Gandhi and Martin Luther King to the environmental movement.' 'We must place our bodies,' he said, 'between the bulldozers and the rain-forest; stand as part of the wilderness in defense of herself; clog the gears of the polluting machine; and with courage oppose the destruction of life:' injunctions Foreman and his group have since carried out at different locations in the American West.

In Europe too, techniques of civil disobedience have come back into fashion among a section of environmentalists. An anti-road campaign in Britain, gathering momentum as I write, has protected old houses, forests and farms by blocking bulldozers and setting up protest camps. These militants seek to defend not an undisturbed wilderness but a composite rural culture remembered and honored in collective memory. But like Dave Foreman, anti-road protesters also acknowledge Gandhi to be a powerful influence—the 'fundamentals of his teachings form the backbone of my beliefs today,' to quote the British campaigner Chris Maile. Foreman and Maile are inspired by Gandhi, but we know that the Mahatma's strategies of civil disobedience were inspired in turn by an essay of Henry David Thoreau, and that his defense of the rural community drew abundantly on the works of John Ruskin and Edward Carpenter. The ideas and example of Gandhi have thus helped return these American and British radicals to their own half-forgotten traditions of dissent and moral authority: testimony, once more, to the global and cross-cultural character of the environmental movement.

RADICAL AMERICAN ENVIRONMENTALISM

In the lexicon of social movements, 'radical' is invariably opposed to 'reformist,' the latter standing for compromise and accommodation, the former for purity and militancy. The word is almost always used in self-definition by thinkers or activists who wish to distinguish themselves from trends they deride as less daring or more compromising than themselves.

In the context of American environmentalism, there are at least two legitimate claimants to the 'radical' label. The first is the strand in the wilderness movement known as 'Deep Ecology.' This dates its origins to an essay published in 1972 by the Norwegian Arné Naess, which called for environmentalists to embrace an ethic, termed *biospheric egalitarianism*, that would place humans on a more or less equal footing with other species. Biospheric egalitarianism would be a truly 'deep' ecology, in contrast to the 'shallow' ecology which concerned itself merely with pollution or resource depletion without going to the deeper roots of the ecological crisis (see *box*). Recast in philosophical terms, this can be stated as the distinction between *anthropocentrism*, the belief that humans stand apart and above the rest of creation, and *biocentrism*, which rejects a human-centered perspective by looking at history from the perspective of other species and nature as a whole.

Naess' work has been controversial in his native Norway, where his campaign for the protection of wolves has angered farmers and his support for the ban on whaling alienated fisherfolk. Indeed, it

---

A PLATFORM FOR DEEP ECOLOGY

Arné Naess offers a set of eight principles for uniting deep ecologists: a platform first outlined by him in 1984 and revised several times since. This version is from 1993.

1. The flourishing of human and nonhuman living beings has intrinsic worth. The worth of nonhuman beings is independent of their usefulness for human purposes.

2. Richness and diversity of life forms on earth, including forms of human cultures, have intrinsic worth.

3. Humans have no right to reduce this richness and diversity, except to satisfy vital needs.

4. The flourishing of human life and cultures is compatible with a substantially smaller human population.

5. Present human interference with the nonhuman world is excessive, and the situation is worsening.

6. The foregoing points indicate that changes are necessary in the dominant way humans until now have behaved in their relation to the earth as a whole. The changes will, in a fundamental manner, affect political, social, technological, economic, and ideological structures.

7. The ideological change in the rich countries will mainly be that of increased appreciation of life quality rather than high material standard of living, in this way preparing [the way for] a global state of ecologically sustainable development.

8. Those who subscribe to the foregoing points have an obligation, directly or indirectly, to try to implement the necessary changes by nonviolent means.

Source: David Rothenberg, *Is it too Painful to Think? Conversations with Arné Naess* (Minneapolis: University of Minnesota Press, 1993), pp. 127–8.

might be said that the most faithful and energetic of his disciples are now to be found in and around the state of California. In the U.S., there already existed a tradition of reflection and activism in defense of the wilderness, a tradition that despite its submergence in the '40s and '50s was being discovered anew (see *box*). In 1967 Roderick Nash published his *Wilderness and the American Mind*, a book that re-presented the ideas of Muir and Leopold to a modern public. A steady stream of Muir biographies followed, and when Oxford University Press brought out a new edition of Leopold's *A Sand County Almanac* in 1973, it sold fifty times as many copies as had the original.

ON HOW THE FIRST WAVE OF WILDERNESS THINKING IS INTEGRATED WITH THE SECOND

A historical geographer's perceptive analysis of why Aldo Leopold's ideas resonate so deeply with the wilderness lovers of the present day:

Leopold's land ethic is immensely popular among purists because it successfully resolves four difficulties. First, the purist is encouraged to see himself as part of the advance guard for a higher level of civilization, which is a much more pleasant self-image than 'nature nut.' Second, Leopold's views on wilderness as a baseline fit very well with the axiom and corollaries of the wilderness ethic. Third, Leopold's fusion of the land ethic with the science of ecology lends the prestige of science to the purist's beliefs. Fourth and most important, geopietistic mystic experience gains a code of moral directives based on scientific fact . . . Science is used to justify the purist's numinous experience and to interpret this experience as a useful, satisfying moral code.

Source: Linda H. Graber, *Wilderness as Sacred Space* (Washington, D.C.: The Association of American Geographers, 1976), p. 50.

Arné Naess' distinction between shallow and deep ecology fitted well with this rediscovery of John Muir and company. It seemed to give a firm philosophical basis to the belief, already widespread among wilderness lovers, that the presence of humans was always and invariably a threat to other species. Deep Ecology found adherents within the scholarly community, with fine-grained discussions of the anthropocentric/biocentric distinction appearing in the scholarly literature. A new and influential journal, *Environmental Ethics*, placed the debate squarely in the center of the academic discipline of philosophy. Beyond the university, Deep Ecology was enthusiastically taken up by activists disenchanted by the gentle lobbying efforts of the Washington professionals. It influence is visible in the very title of Earth First!, the group that has most stridently captured this disaffection with incremental methods to protect nature. Elsewhere in the forests of North America, militant efforts to defend the wild have also been inspired by the tenets of Deep Ecology. One such place is the Canadian province of British Columbia where, as Catherine Caufield writes, radicals have

> blockaded logging roads with fallen trees, boulders and their own bodies; buried themselves up to their necks in the paths of advancing bulldozers, and suspended themselves from trees, dangling a hundred feet off the ground for days at a time. Less frequently, they have engaged in controversial acts of sabotage, ranging from pouring sugar into the gasoline tanks of logging trucks, to disabling bulldozers, to rendering trees worthless—and dangerous—for milling by driving six-inch-long iron spikes into them.

These actions are mandated by the ethic that the interests of nature are as important as the interests of humans: that to put yourself in the path of an advancing bulldozer is to invoke the most radical traditions of philosophical thought and environmental action. Deep Ecologists, whether within the academy or outside it, see themselves as the intellectual, spiritual and political vanguard of American environmentalism. But this self definition has not gone uncontested. Its critics accuse it of misanthropy and of a peculiar blindness of its own, which ignores environmental degradation outside the wild and the human suffering that is its consequence. Deep Ecologists are charged, with some reason, for ignoring the problems of social inequality, both within the countries of the North and between the North and the South. Within the United States itself, the wilderness movement has scorned the city, which it sees as the source of all that is modern, industrial, man-made, and hence *un*natural. Indeed, as the sociologist Michael Meyerfeld Bell has pointed out, much of contemporary environmentalism derives from an 'ideology of urban abandonment and urban escape', resulting in a near-complete neglect of the ecological problems of city life. The critics of Deep Ecology draw attention to another and in their view more authentically radical strand, the *environmental justice* movement.

Where the nerve-centers of Deep Ecology are in the wild, environmental justice is firmly rooted in human habitations. The threats it fears are toxic waste dumps and landfills, the excretions of affluence that have to be disposed of somehow, and somewhere. An early and notorious case is of the unhappily named Love Canal in upstate

New York, the recipient of 43 million pounds of wastes produced by the firm of Hooker Chemicals.

Love Canal happens to pass through a white area, but other toxic waste sites have been overwhelmingly located in areas inhabited by minority communities. For example, more than 2 million tons of uranium tailings have been thrown onto Native American lands, in some cases causing rates of cancer twenty times the national average. Likewise, a study commissioned by the National Assocation for the Advancement of Colored Peoples estimates that almost 60 per cent of all African-Americans have been put at risk by hazardous waste dumps and landfills. The Alabama town of Emelle, whose population is four-fifths Black, receives wastes from all of forty-five states.

One of the first to blow the whistle on this process of effluent discrimination was the sociologist Robert Bullard. He found that in the city of Houston, where Whites comfortably outnumber Blacks, three out of four disposal sites had been placed in black neighborhoods. Bullard saw that 'the landfill question appears to have galvanized and politicized a part of the Houston community, the Black community, which for years had been inactive on environmental issues.' Indeed, movements of resistance to dangerous dump-sites have sprung up in numerous towns and counties across America. Lois Gibbs, who led the campaign to clean up Love Canal, helped set up a national co-ordinating body, the Citizens Clearinghouse for Hazardous Wastes (CCHW), which lists a staggering 4000 affiliated groups. Through demonstrations, press campaigns and lawsuits, these groups have worked to stop fresh sitings or have made industry and government accountable for the hazards posed by dumps that already exist.

These struggles are currently being chronicled by sociologists, but early reports from the battlefield all point to one striking feature: the leading role of women. The opposition to polluters has often been in the hands of housewives with no previous experience of social activism. Within the communities where wastes are being dumped, men are sometimes susceptible to blandishments of job or money, but women do not see the health of their children as a 'negotiable category.' A resister in southern Los Angeles explained her opposition to an incinerator thus: 'People's jobs were threatened, ministers were threatened, but, I said, "I'm not going to be intimidated." My child's health comes first; that's more important than a job.' Nor has this been purely a defensive operation; led by Lois Gibbs and the CCHW, the movement has also outlined, as alternatives to the production and dispersal of toxics, the 'four R's of recycling, reduction, reuse and reclamation.'

The struggles against hazardous wastes have contributed to a profound reorientation of American environmentalism. The political scientist Ken Geiser suggests that because the anti-toxics movement is 'so tightly rooted in the immediate experience of people's community and family life, it has an urgency and concreteness that is incredibly compelling.' The movement, he further notes, is composed largely of 'working-class and other lower-income people who would feel out of place at a meeting of a typical chapter of say, the Audobon Society or the Sierra Club.' For these 'new' environmentalists, the 'environment is not an abstract concept polluted and decreasing in beauty and scientific value. For many [of them] it is something which has already exposed them to hazards which are debilitating them and hastening their deaths.' Or, as an African-American activist more simply and sharply put it: 'The principle of social justice must be at the heart of any effort aimed at bringing Blacks into the mainstream of environmental organizations in the U. S. [We] must not misuse concern for endangered species as a way of diluting our responsibility to meet [the] basic need for human health care, food and shelter.'

THE GERMAN GREENS

Environmentalists of all kinds are now known as 'greens,' much as socialists of different tendencies were once known as 'reds.' The color has come to stand for nature, for life; its association with environmentalism so firmly rooted in the popular mind that in this book I have used it unselfconsciously and ubiquitously. Yet the usage is of surpisingly recent provenance. It dates to 1978, when a group of environmentalists taking part in local elections in Germany put forward candidates under the 'Green List,' *Grüne Liste Umweltschutz*. From that modest beginning arose a national party to which the label attached itself. It is this party and its later and conspicuous successes which have led to the identification of the color green with environmentalists in Germany, and everywhere else.

Formed in March 1979, the Green Party made a stunning entry into the Bundestag in the elections of 1983, the first new party to 'make it' to the German Parliament in sixty years. Its position was consolidated in the elections of 1987, and after a poor performance in the post-unification polls of 1990, in the 1994 elections as well. By this time Greens were also represented in most provincial parliaments, and even held office (in coalition with the social democratic party, the SPD) in one or two provinces. The German Greens offered a beacon for environmentalists in other European countries, who tried to form political parties of their own. It has been a hard act to follow, and although in Belgium, Italy and Sweden green parties have since entered Parliament, they have not had quite the same impact. In the history of modern environmentalism, the German Greens stand out for their political victories and for the moral challenge they offer to the governing beliefs of industrial civilization.

The origins of the Greens can be traced, at one remove, to the efflorescence all over the North Atlantic world of social movements in the 1960s. After the end of the Second World War the German people had turned inward, persuaded by the ruling Christian Democratic Union to forget their horrific immediate past and work collectively toward the good, i.e. affluent, society. Chancellors Konrad Adenauer and Ludwig Erhard ruled over a nationwide consensus to the effect that political stability would generate prosperity. In the late '60s, however, a militant student movement sprung up, which used the Vietnam war to mount a more general broadside against authority and the 'Establishment.' Simultaneous with the students' struggle were a series of citizens' actions, the so-called *Burger Initiativen* (BI), which for the first time in recent German history expressed an open skepticism of parties, politicians, and the state.

As in neighboring France and England, the protest of the students was at first captured in the number 1968, denoting a year, a mood, and a movement. The students' revolt played itself out in a while, but the BIs were rather more enduring. The Indian scholar Saral Sarkar, a longtime resident of Germany and a keen observer of its politics, suggests that the BIs passed through three distinct if chronologically overlapping phases. From 1969 to 1972 they operated mostly as 'one-point actions,' a multitude of local efforts to stop damaging industries, rehabilitate battered women and drug addicts, and construct playgrounds and schools without waiting for the government to do so. At this time the BIs took up a wide array of causes before finding 'its predominant theme in ecology.' This sharpening of focus was helped along by the formation, in Frankfurt in 1972, of a federal union of BIs, with more than a thousand registered groups and a membership of over 300,000 individuals.

The controversy over nuclear power emerged as central to this redefinition of a dispersed network of citizens' initiatives as the 'ecology movement.' Following the oil price hike of 1973, West Germany embarked upon an ambitious—but to many citizens reckless—expansion of its nuclear industry. New plants were feared for their contributions to pollution, for their links to the armanents industry, and for the shroud of secrecy which surrounded them. Opposition to atomic energy as a 'sellout of the future' brought under one banner farmers whose lands and homes would have to make way for the new nuclear power plants with the educated middle-class of the cities, for whom this risky and potentially lethal technology became the 'very embodiment of socio-economic development gone wrong.' 'The fear of the people,' wrote a Hamburg correspondent in November 1973,

> is today ranged not only against the danger from nuclear power plants themselves, but primarily against the industrial concentrations which are necessarily connected with the massive energy production. . . . If the unrestrained industrial growth is not stopped, then in the course of the next few years we shall experience the destruction of our ecology and with it the poisoning of the water and air of Hamburg in an un-precedented and unimaginable scale. It would not suffice any more to see "environmental protection" in protests against carelessly thrown away banana skins.

As elsewhere, protesters against polluting industries took readily to the streets. The '70s in Germany were peppered with demonstra-tions and strikes against new nuclear plants and older chemical fact-ories. Keeping pace with civil disobedience were the writings of intellectuals who promoted a society greener than the one they found themselves in. When the established political parties continued to keep their distance, environmentalists thought of directly represent-ing themselves. From 1977 they began putting up candidates at local and municipal elections. These regional efforts crystallized in an 'al-ternative political alliance,' or what we now know as the Green Party.

In the new formation from the beginning was Petra Kelly, a young and highly personable woman of mixed German-American parent-age. Kelly hoped the party would be 'a lobby for all those who have no lobby.' Others were more specific. The Green Member of Parlia-ment Helmut Lippelt recalled the party as having

> attracted conservatives concerned about protection of the environment; Christians concerned about the destruction of creation; educated liberals who had learned about global ecology; technicians with knowledge of high-risk technologies; socialists concerned about the fallouts of capitalism; and, of course, the new Marxist-Leninists, waiting for the true left party and examining whether perhaps they could educate *Die Grünen* to become just that party.

The journalist Werner Hülsberg provides another exhaustive list-ing, not necessarily incompatible with the first. The party drew into its fold, he writes, 'farmers whose existence was threatened, radical-democratic doctors, left-liberal school teachers, critical trade unionists, bored office workers, young people without any future, radicalized women, nature-lovers, freaked-out hippies, militant animal rightists and a whole host of mueslies (health-food addicts) . . .'

This mother-of-all-rainbow coalitions sent forth some of its members to the Bundestag in 1983, after the Greens had unexpectedly crossed the threshold 5 per cent of the popular vote which qualified them for representation. Their diversity marked them out from the dourly homogeneous parties which sat across them. The most charismatic of the Green MPs, Petra Kelly, thought this was their strength. 'The variety of currents enriches our party,' she remarked, for 'I don't want to exclude communists and conservatives, and I don't have to. One current learns from the other. There is no mutual destruction, but a convergence of views. That's what is new about our movement.'

These hopes were illusory, for a political party needs to be rather more single-minded than a social movement. When the party was faced with the prospect of forming provincial governments with the well-established SPD, the whiff of power brought to the fore an apparently irreconcilable opposition between two groups, dubbed in journalistic shorthand as the Fundis (fundamentalists) and the Realos (or realists). Where the Fundis rejected any thought of Green participation in government, seeing it as the final sell-out to the Establishment, the Realos believed they owed it to their voters to responsibly incorporate Green ideals in governance. The Fundis thought little of parliamentary work, preferring to canvass among local groups and the citizenry at large. The Realos on the other hand welcomed the attention paid by the media to their new and distinctive voice in parliament, and accordingly gave importance to televised speeches as well as to closed-door committee work. These differences in political tactics masked deeper ideological divisions too. Thus the Fundis were wholly opposed to the market, the epitome to them of greed and avarice; the Realos argued that since the market was here to stay the task was to tame and control it, not to turn one's back on it.

The Fundis were, and are, themselves of two kinds, each drawing on a rich historical tradition. On the one side were the socialists-turned-ecologists, colored reddish-green so to speak, contemporary carriers of the German brand of revolutionary communism once associated with such figures as Rosa Luxemburg and Karl Liebnecht. These eco-socialists rejected industrial capitalism but nourished the hope that a future socialist society would be more gentle on the environment (see *box*). On the other side were the agrarian romantics, colored deep green, who offered as their alternative to industrial society the decentralized rural utopia dreamt of by countless German poets down the centuries. But both types of Fundis stood, in the words of the philosopher Rudolf Bahro, for the 'radical reversal of

---

SOME PRECONDITIONS FOR RESOLVING THE ECOLOGY CRISIS

In a talk at Freiburg in 1979, the philosopher Rudolf Bahro, an erstwhile East German dissident who became a leading member of the 'Fundi' faction of the West German Greens, outlined some pretty radical solutions to the ecology crisis. His list makes for an intriguing contrast with the principles outlined by Arné Naess, quoted earlier. While Naess lays more stress on ethical and value change, Bahro, and the German Greens generally, focus somewhat more on changes in existing patterns of production, consumption and distribution.

— The ecology crisis is insoluble unless we work at the same time at overcoming the confrontation of military blocs. It is insoluble without a resolute policy of detente and disarmament, one that renounces all demands for subverting other countries. . . .

— The ecology crisis is insoluble without a new world order on the North-South axis. And we must realize that our entire standard of living [in the North] is largely based on the exploitation and suppression of the rest of humanity. . . .

— The ecology crisis is insoluble without a decisive breakthrough towards social justice in our own country and without a swift equalisation of social differences throughout Western Europe. . . .

— The ecology crisis is insoluble without progress in human emancipation here and now, even while capitalism still exists. It is insoluble without countless individuals managing to rise above their immediate and compensatory interests. . . .

— If all this is brought to a common denominator, the conclusion is as follows: The ecology crisis is insoluble under capitalism. We have to get rid of the capitalist manner of regulating the economy, and above all of the capitalist driving mechanism, for a start at least bringing it under control. In other words, there is no solution to the ecology crisis without the combination of all anti-capitalist and socialist tendencies for a peaceful democratic revolution against the dominant economic structure. . . .

Source: Rudolf Bahro, *Socialism and Survival* (London: Merlin Books, 1982), pp. 41–3.

the capitalist industrial system,' a perspective from which Green participation in government was merely to 'clean the dragon's teeth and
freshen its breath.'

The Fundis gave powerful stimulus to the Green party in its early
years, but over time they found themselves increasingly at odds with
the rank-and-file. An estimated 80 per cent of Green voters wanted
their party to work with the SPD in bringing about legislation to
check pollution and moderate energy use. The Realos found their
most effective spokesman in Joschka Fischer, Green Minister of
Environment in Hesse between 1985 and 1987, a votary of 'qualitat-
ive growth' who sought to temper and redirect industrial society toward a greener path. 'I am no longer motivated by utopias,' remarked
Fischer in 1985, 'but by the description of existing conditions. The
ecological crisis, the arms race, the rise in criminality—those are more
than enough for me. I am no missionary with a promise of a new
tomorrow . . . If we can take one step in the right direction, one step
which moves us away from the abyss, then that is sufficient justifica-
tion for the existence of the [party].' The language, consciously or
unconsciously, is reminscient of Mahatma Gandhi's, likewise a politician who combined a utopian vision with shrewdly practical ends,
who liked to speak of the 'beauty of compromise' and of 'taking one
step at a time.'

At the time of writing the Realos reign triumphant, with Fischer
himself being one of the best-known and popular German politicians. Knowledgeable analysts accurately predicted the prospect of a
SPD–Green coalition capturing the Bundestag in the 1998 election,
thus ending nearly twenty years of rule by the conservative Christian Democratic Union. Three Greens have joined the Cabinet, with
Joschka Fischer appointed the new Foreign Minister of the most
populous, most prosperous and most influential country in Europe.
This surely marks the highest point of a journey already singular in
the history of global environmentalism. But let me conclude this assessment by asking, first: Why did the Greens rise to prominence in
Germany and nowhere else? And second, what in the ideas of the
German Greens is of real and lasting significance?

Why is there no Green party in my country, the American reader
will ask. In fact there is one, founded in Minneapolis in 1984, but
with little to show in the thirteen years it has been around. One hurdle
the American Green Party faces is the vibrant presence of apolitical
environmental groups such as the Sierra Club and the Wilderness
Society, who seem already to have captured the loyalty of the environmentalist constituency. Another is the entrenched two-party

system, in which better equipped 'third' parties—the Socialists of Norman Thomas, the Progressives led by Henry Wallace, the Populists of George Wallace, and most recently Ross Perot's Reform Party—have failed to make a dent. The Federal Republic of Germany also has two dominant parties of its own—the CDU and the SPD—but smaller parties are given a decent chance by the system of proportional representation, through which a group commanding more than 5 per cent of the vote can enter Parliament. Proportional representation has allowed environmentalists to take the political route in Germany, an option foreclosed by the constituency-based system prevalent in countries such as the U.S. and the U.K.

To this political difference one must add a geographical one, viz. that West Germany was a front-line state in the Cold War. It faced the massed might of the Soviets across the Iron Curtain and was the unwilling home of thousands of NATO troops and their nuclear weapons. Germans were hence able to more starkly perceive the destructive power of industrial society—as compared, for instance, to isolated Canadians or insulated residents of the state of California—and to more readily embrace a caring attitude towards the earth. Not to be discounted either was the Nazi past, which has fostered a massive guilt complex among the ordinary and especially the educated German, an urgent and overpowering desire to atone for the crimes of a previous generation. This has unquestionably heightened their sense of responsibility to other cultures and later generations. Taking the idea of 'Limits to Growth' seriously, they have turned the searchlight inward, illuminating the ways in which their society sets an unworthy example to the rest of the world. 'The key to a sustainable development model worldwide,' writes Helmut Lippelt, 'is the question of whether West European societies really are able to reconstruct their industrial systems in order to permit an ecologically and socially viable way of production and consumption.' That Lippelt does not include the U.S. or Japan is noteworthy, an expression of his, and his movement's, willingness to take the burden upon themselves. West Europeans should reform themselves, rather than transfer their existing 'patterns of high production and high consumption to eastern Europe and the "Third World" [and thus] destroy the earth.'

For the German Greens, economic growth in Europe and North America has been made possible only through the economic and ecological exploitation of the Third World. Rudolf Bahro is characteristically blunt: 'the present way of life of the most industrially advanced nations,' he says, 'stands in a global and antagonistic contradiction to the natural conditions of human existence. We are eating up what other nations and future generations need to live on.' From this perspective, indeed—

> The working class here [in the North] is the richest lower class in the world. And if I look at the problem from the point of view of the whole of humanity, not just from that of Europe, then I must say that the metropolitan working class is the worst exploiting class in history. . . What made poverty bearable in eighteenth or nineteenth-century Europe was the prospect of escaping it through exploitation of the periphery. But this is no longer a possibility, and continued industrialism in the Third World will mean poverty for whole generations and hunger for millions.

Even the most hardheaded Realo acknowledges the unsustainability, on the global plane, of industrial society. Joschka Fischer, asked by a reporter where he planned to spend his old age, replied: 'In the Frankfurt cemetery, although by that time we may pose an environmental hazard with all the poisons, heavy metals and dioxin that we carry around in our bodies.' Or as a party document more matter-of-factly put it: 'The global spread of industrial economic policies and lifestyles is exhausting the basic ecological health of our planet faster than it can be replenished.' This global view, coupled with the stress on accountability, calls for 'far-reaching *voluntary* commitments to restraint by wealthy nations.' The industrialized countries, which consume three-fourths of the world's energy and resources, and who contribute the lion's share of 'climate-threatening gaseous emissions,' must curb their voracious appetite while allowing Southern nations to grow out of poverty. The Greens ask for the cancellation of all international debt, the banning of trade in products that destroy vulnerable ecosystems, and, most radical of all, for the freer migration of peoples from poor countries to rich ones.

Attentive to the rights of other nations and future generations, the Greens have also taken aboard the claims of the most disadvantaged section of their own society: women. By party mandate, fully 50 per cent of all officers and parliamentarians have to be women. During meetings and congresses, the roster alternates men and women speakers, rather than simply leave the floor open to those who are more aggressive or have louder voices (who would most likely be men). These policies had immediate results, with the number of women who voted for the Party increasing six-fold between 1980 and 1987. But Green feminism is not restricted to public fora: thus a 'Mothers' Manifesto' presented to the party has urged that the traditional concern with equal pay for equal work be enlarged to properly compensate housewives who contribute, unpaid, roughly half of all social labor. It is these mothers, moreover, who have taken the lead in organizing 'ecologically responsible households.'

Their feminism in theory and in practice adds to the list of what marks the Greens out as the most daring political experiment of our times. When they appeared on the German stage a decade or more ago, the famously conservative prime minister of Bavaria, Franz-Josef Strauss, dismissed them as 'the Trojan horse of the Soviet cavalry.' But now even Strauss' CDU party has borrowed elements of the Green program, proof of the party's impact on the most recalcitrant of its opponents. For all their 'various shortcomings and difficulties,' notes the political scientist Margit Mayer, the Green Party has

> transformed the political landscape of Germany. What used to be considered nonconventional, marginal and utopian demands of the Greens in the '70s—such as demands to end nuclear energy, end linear economic growth, bring about unilateral disarmament, or proportional representation of women in all spheres—are now discussed and even demanded by other parties in the political mainstream.

Mayer writes only of the impact in Germany, but of course the party has attracted considerable attention and acclaim all over the globe. It might justly be regarded as the finest achievement of the second wave of environmentalism, referred to by the respectful capital that sets it apart from its peers and contemporaries: the Greens, as distinct from all other kinds of greens.

6

The Southern Challenge

There is a widespread belief that environmentalism is a phenomenon peculiar to the rich nations of the North, a product of the move toward 'postmaterialist' values among the populations of North America and Western Europe. In a series of books and essays published over the last twenty years, the political scientist Ronald Inglehart has argued that environmentalism is central to this shift 'from giving top priority to physical sustenance and safety toward heavier emphasis on belonging, self-expression, and the quality of life.' A corollary of this thesis is the claim that poor countries cannot possibly generate environmental movements of their own. Consider these statements by three senior, serious scholars:

> If you look at the countries that are interested in environmentalism, or at the individuals who support environmentalism within each country, one is struck by the extent to which environmentalism is an interest of the upper middle class. Poor countries and poor individuals simply aren't interested. (Lester Thurow, *The Zero-Sum Society*, 1980).

> It is no accident that the main support for ecological policies comes from the rich countries and from the comfortable rich and middle classes (except for businessmen, who hope to make money by polluting activity). The poor, multiplying and under-employed, wanted more 'development,' not less. (Eric Hobsbawm, *The Age of Extremes*, 1994).

> Only the maligned Western world has the money and the will to conserve its environment. It is the 'Northern White Empire's' last burden, and may be its last crusade. (Anna Bramwell, *The Fading of the Greens*, 1994).

From this point of view, the expression of environmentalism in countries not previously marked by it is a sign that these societies have finally arrived at the threshold of modernity and affluence. When protests against pollution broke out near Seoul in 1991, the respected British weekly, the *New Scientist*, announced that South Korea had at last 'woken up to the environment.' Likewise, the steady growth of an environmental constituency in Taiwan has been interpreted as a consequence of the clear triumph, within that island nation, of modernity over tradition. The Taiwanese, writes Stevan Harrell, had come to—

> value nature because the city is polluted and noisy, and because nature is more accessible than it was. They go on [excursions on] weekends because their time, as industrial citizens, is structured in regular blocks. . . . There is nothing particularly Chinese about any of this, nor is there anything particularly Western or Westernized. There is something peculiarly modern, the self-critique of the social formation that has allowed all this leisure and luxury.

By equating environmentalism exclusively with affluence, scholars seem to posit an evolutionary sequence—of poor societies becoming prosperous before they can find green movements in their midst. But as Steven Brechin and Willett Kempton note, 'the conventional wisdom—that the citizens of developing countries do not or cannot care about the environment—has been broadly accepted by Western publics and the diplomatic community, with theoretical backing from the postmaterialist thesis but *with little data from those developing countries.*'

The consensus that *Silent Spring* begat the modern environmental movement might be allowed to stand; but the consensus that the societies of the Third World are too poor to be green shall not go undisputed. By bringing in 'data from those developing countries,' this chapter suggests that there does in fact exist a vibrant and growing environmental constituency in societies such as Brazil, India and Thailand, countries far-flung and richly varied among themselves but united nonetheless by the poverty of the masses of their peoples.

THE ENVIRONMENTALISM OF THE POOR

Let me offer five examples of poor peoples' environmentalism, taken from five recognizably less-than-wealthy societies of the globe.

1. The Penan are a tiny community of hunters and farmers who live in the forests of the Malaysian state of Sarawak. They number

less than 7000 individuals, and do not generally seek the limelight. In the late '80s, however, they became major players in a major controversy. For their forest home had been steadily encroached upon by commercial loggers, whose felling activities had fouled their rivers, exposed their soils and destroyed plants and animals which they harvested for food. Beyond this material loss was a deeper loss of meaning, for the Penan have a strong cultural bond with their river and forest landscape. Helped by Bruno Manser, a Swiss artist who then lived with them, the tribe organized blockades and demonstrations to force the chainsaws and their operators back to where they came from. The Penan struggle was taken up and publicized by the respected Penang-based group, Sahabat Alam Malaysia, and by transnational forums such as Greenpeace and the Rainforest Action Network.

2. The Sardar Sarovar dam, being built on the Narmada river in central India, shall stand as a showpiece of Indian economic development. Four hundred and sixty feet high when completed, the dam will provide much-needed irrigation and electricity, but it shall also submerge historic old temples, rich deciduous forests, and at least 250 villages. These potential 'oustees' have come together under the banner of the Narmada Bachao Andolan (Save the Narmada Movement), which is led by a forty-year-old woman, Medha Patkar. In their bid to stop dam construction, Patkar and her colleagues have fasted outside provincial legislatures, camped outside the Indian prime minister's house in New Delhi, and walked through the Narmada valley to raise awareness of the predicament of the to-be-displaced villagers.

3. Pressed to earn foreign exchange, the state forest department of Thailand initiated, in the late '70s, the conversion of acres and acres of natural forests into monocultural plantations of eucalyptus. The department hopes to thus plant up 60,000 square kilometres by the year 2020, to provide eucalyptus chips for paper mills, mostly owned by Japanese companies. While bureaucrats in Bangkok contemplated a rising intake of yen, peasants in the forests began opposition to the plantations. They believed that their rice fields would be affected by the proximity of the water-guzzling and soil-depleting Australian tree; they also mourned the loss of the mixed forests from which they harvested fodder, fuel, fruit and medicines. Peasant protesters are mobilized by Buddhist priests, who lead delegations to public officials and also conduct 'ordination' ceremonies to prevent natural forests being turned into artificial ones.

4. On November 10, 1995, the military dictatorship of Nigeria hung nine dissenters, the most prominent of whom was the poet and

Medha Patkar, leader of the Narmada Bachao Andolan (Save Narmada Movement), addressing a public meeting in Mumbai in 1992.

SOURCE Frontline *magazine.*

playwright Ken Saro-Wiwa. Their crime had been to draw attention
to the impact on their Ogoni tribe of oil drilling by the Anglo-Dutch
conglomerate, Royal Shell. Shell had been drawing some 25,000 bar-
rels a day from the Ogoni territories. The federal government bene-
fited from oil exploration in the form of rising revenues, but the
Ogoni lost a great deal. They remained without schools, or hospitals;
thirty-five years of drilling had instead led to death and devastation:
'a blighted countryside, an atmosphere full of . . . carbon monoxide
and hydrocarbon; a land in which wildlife is unknown; a land of polluted streams and creeks, a land which is, in every sense of the term,
an ecological disaster.' The Movement for the Survival of the Ogoni
People, founded by Saro-Wiwa in 1991, had intensified the public
opposition to Shell and its military backers. The generals in Lagos
responded with threats, intimidation, arrest, and finally by judicially
murdering Saro-Wiwa and his colleagues.

5. My final illustration is one of environmental reconstruction
rather than protest. This is Kenya's Green Belt Movement, founded
by Waangari Matthai, an anatomist schooled at the University of Kan-
sas who became her country's first woman professor. In 1977 Matthai
threw up her university position to motivate other, less-privileged
women to protect and improve their environment. Starting with a
mere seven saplings planted on June 5, 1977 (World Environment
Day), the movement had by 1992 distributed 7,000,000 saplings, planted and cared for by groups of village women spread over twenty-two
districts of Kenya. The Green Belt Movement, writes the journalist
Fred Pearce, has 'arguably done more to stall the expansion of deserts
and the destruction of soils in Africa than its big brother international body down the road, the United Nations Environmental Program [also headquartered in Nairobi] with its grand but largely unsuccessful anti-desertification programs.'

The cases I have chosen are all moderately well known among
the environmental community. Medha Patkar was honored with the
prestigious Goldman award (endowed by California philanthropists);
the Penan have had films about their plight broadcast on British and
German television; Saro-Wiwa's death even made it to the front page
of the staid *New York Times*. I could certainly have chosen better
known examples of the environmentalism of the poor: indeed two
such, possibly the most famous of all, are examined later in the chapter. But I could also have chosen lesser-known examples, which number in the hundreds in the countries of the South. These include other
movements that oppose commercial logging and industrial monocultures while defending traditional community rights and natural

Waangari Matthai, founder of the Kenyan Green Belt Movement.

SOURCE Photo by Runar Malkenes, here taken from Fred Pearce, The Green Warriors *(The Bodley Head).*

forests; other struggles of dam-displaced people who do not wish to make way for expensive and destructive 'mega-projects;' movements of peasants whose crops and pastureland have been destroyed by limestone mines or granite quarries; movements of artisanal fisherfolk directed at modern high-tech trawlers that destroy their livelihood even as they deplete fish stocks; and movements against paper factories by communities living downstream, for whom chemical effluents destroy the beauty of the river as well as their sole source of drinking water. To these struggles against environmental degradation one must add struggles for environmental renewal, the numerous and growing efforts by rural communities in Asia and Africa to better manage their forests, conserve their soil, sustainably harvest their water or use energy-saving devices like improved stoves and biogas plants.

'The environmentalism of the poor' is a convenient umbrella term that I shall use for these varied forms of social action. The Peruvian activist Hugo Blanco has evocatively distinguished this kind of environmentalism from its better known and more closely studied Northern counterpart. At first sight, writes Blanco,

> environmentalists or conservationists are nice, slightly crazy guys whose main purpose in life is to prevent the disappearance of blue whales or pandas. The common people have more important things to think about, for instance how to get their daily bread. Sometimes they are taken to be not so crazy but rather smart guys who, in the guise of protecting endangered species, have formed so-called NGOs to get juicy amounts of dollars from abroad . . . Such views are sometimes true. However, there are in Peru a very large number of people who are environmentalists. Of course, if I tell such people, you are ecologists, they might reply, 'ecologist your mother,' or words to that effect. Let us see, however. Isn't the village of Bambamarca truly environmentalist, which has time and again fought valiantly against the pollution of its water from mining? Are not the town of Ilo and the surrounding villages which are being polluted by the Southern Peru Copper Corporation truly environmentalist? Is not the village of Tambo Grande in Piura environmentalist when it rises like a closed fist and is ready to die in order to prevent strip-mining in its valley? Also, the people of the Mantaro Valley who saw their little sheep die, because of the smoke and waste from La Oroya smelter. And the population of Amazonia, who are totally environmentalist, and die defending their forests against depredation. Also the poor people of Lima are environmentalists, when they complain against the pollution of water in the beaches.

> [translated from the Spanish by Juan Martinez Alier]

One can identify some half-a-dozen distinguishing features of the environmentalism of the poor. First and foremost, it combines a concern for the environment with an often more visible concern for social justice. Through much of the Third World, writes David Cleary, 'reality is a seamless web of social and environmental constraints which it makes little sense to atomise into mutually exclusive categories.' Commercial forestry, oil drilling, and large dams all damage the environment, but they also, and to their victims more painfully, constitute a threat to rural livelihoods: by depriving tribals of fuelwood and small game, by destroying the crops of farmers, or by submerging wholesale the lands and homes of villagers who have the misfortune to be placed in their path. The opposition to these interventions is thus as much a defense of livelihood as an 'environmental' movement in the narrow sense of the term. This inseparability of social and environmental concerns is beautifully captured in a petition of December 1990, addressed to the President of Mexico by a community of Nahuatl Indians who were asked to make way for the proposed San Juan dam on the Balsa river:

> Mr President., we publicly and collectively declare our rejection of the San Juan Telecingo Dam because we cannot allow this project to destroy the economy, the historical and cultural heritage, and the natural resources on which [we] depend . . . This project, by flooding our villages and our lands, would cause great losses and hardships to us in every way: we would lose our houses, churches, town halls, roads, irrigation systems and other collective works that we have undertaken with great sacrifice over many years. We would lose the best farmland that we live from; we would lose the pastures that support our livestock; we would lose our orchards and our fruit trees; we would lose the clay deposits and other raw materials we use for our crafts; we would lose our cemeteries where our dead are buried, our churches, and the caves, springs and other sacred places where we make our offerings; we would lose, among others, Teopantecuanitlan, a unique archeological site of great importance . . .; we would lose all the natural resources we know and use for our sustenance as taught to us by our ancestors. We would lose so many things that we cannot express them all here because we would never finish this document.

> [translated from the Spanish by Catherine Good]

The fact that environmental degradation often intensifies *economic* deprivation explains the moral urgency of these movements of protest. The anthropologist Peter Brosius has seen in the Penan struggle an 'unambiguous statement of the rightness of one's case;' but similarly convinced that right—though not necessarily might—is on their side are the rural communities who oppose eucalyptus plantations, polluting factories, or soil-exposing mines. There too, a longstanding, *prior* claim to the resource in question—land, water, forests, fish— has been abruptly extinguished by profiteers working in concert with government, which has granted these outsiders oil, mineral or logging concessions. There is then manifest a palpable sense of betrayal, a feeling that the government, *their* government, has let down the poor by taking the side of the rich. For the Penan, notes Brosius, government officials have become 'men who don't know how to pity . . .;' men 'unfeeling about creating such hardship and disregardful of their concerns.'

There is, however, at first the hope that the government will come to see the error of its ways. These struggles thus most often begin by addressing letters and petitions to persons of authority, themselves in a position to bring about remedial action. It is when these pleas are unanswered that protesters turn to more direct forms of confrontation. Unlike in the North, where electronic media and direct mailers are intelligently used to canvass support, the channels of communication in the South rely rather more heavily on 'traditional' networks such as village and tribe, lineage and caste. Once a sufficient number of like-minded people have been gathered together, there unfolds a richly varied repertoire of collective action. In a study of popular environmentalism in India, I was able to identify seven distinct forms of social protest. These were the *dharna* or sit-down strike; the *pradarshan* or massed procession; the *hartal* or general strike (forcing shops to down shutters); the *rasta roko* or transport blockade (by squatting on rail tracks or highways); the *bhook hartal* or hunger fast (conducted at a strategic site, say the office of the dam engineer, and generally by a recognized leader of the movement); the *gherao*, which is to surround an office or official for days on end; and the *jail bharo andolan* or movement to fill jails by the collective breach of a law considered unjust.

Most of these methods were perfected by Mahatma Gandhi in his battles with British colonialism, but of course they have ready equivalents in other peasant cultures. Larry Lohmann, writing of the opposition to eucalyptus in rural Thailand, remarks on how—

> Small-scale farmers are weathering the contempt of bureaucrats and petitioning district officials and cabinet ministers, standing up to assassination threats and arranging strategy meetings with villagers from other areas. They are holding rallies, speaking out at seminars, blocking roads, and marching on government offices, singing songs composed

for the occasion. Where other means fail and they are well enough organized, they are ripping out eucalyptus seedlings, either surreptitiously or openly in large mobs, chopping down eucalyptus trees, stopping bulldozers and burning nurseries and equipment. At the same time, well aware of the need to seize the environmentalist high ground, many villagers are planting fruit, rubber, and native forest trees to preempt or replace eucalyptus and are explaining to sympathetic journalists the methods they have used to preserve local forest patches for generations.

These protests, singly and collectively, are sometimes underwritten by a powerful indigenous ideology of social justice. Gandhi, for instance, has given Indian environmentalists their most favored techniques of protest as well as a moral vocabulary to oppose the destruction of the village economy by industrialization. Thai peasants, likewise, take recourse to the Buddha and Buddhism to remind their rulers, who publicly profess the same religion, that their policies are a clear violation of the creedal commitment to justice, moderation and harmony with nature. It is notable that the anti-eucalyptus struggle has been led by Buddhist priests, known appositely as *phra nakanu-raksa,* or 'ecology monks.' In Latin America, the ideology most conveniently at hand is popular Catholicism and its contemporary variant, 'liberation theology,' which makes clear the mandate of the clergy, and of the church as a whole, to redirect its energies towards the poor. Thus the resisters to the San Juan dam asked parish priests to hold nightly prayer meetings, walked with images of village patron saints to the site of the dam, and also marched to the cathedral in Mexico City in honor of the hallowed Virgin of Guadalupe.

One striking feature of the environmentalism of the poor has been the significant and sometimes determining part played by women. Women have effortlessly assumed leadership roles—as with Medha Patkar or Waangari Matthai, for example—and also contributed more than their fair share to making up the numbers in marches and demonstrations, strikes and fasts. They have been unafraid, in an often brutal political culture, of being harrassed, beaten or jailed. When a Venezuelan feminist writes that in her country 'today all women's groups are environmentalist regardless of whether they know what the environment means,' she could be speaking for women in India or Malaysia, Brazil, Kenya and Mexico.

Among women in the countryside, certainly, there is often a deep awareness of the dependence of human society on a clean and bountiful environment. A tribal woman in the Bastar district of central India, herself active in a forest protection campaign, puts it this way:

'What will happen if there are no forests? *Bhagwan Mahaprabhu* [God] and *Dharti Maata* [Mother Earth] will leave our side, they will leave us and we will die. It is because the earth exists that we are sitting here and talking.' Inspired by such remarks, some feminist scholars posit a near-mystical bond between women and nature, an intrinsic and proto-biological rapport which in their view is denied to men. Other feminists have argued, in my view more plausibly, that the participation of women in environmental movements stems from their closer day-to-day involvement in the use of nature, and additionally from their greater awareness and respect for community cohesion and solidarity. In the divison of labor typical of most peasant, tribal and pastoralist households, it falls on women (and children) to gather fuelwood, collect water, and harvest edible plants. They are thus more easily able to perceive, and more quickly respond to, the drying up of springs or the disappearance of forests. But it is also the case that women, more than men, are inclined to the long view, to sense, for example, that eucalyptus planted for industry might bring in some quick cash today but will undermine their economic security for tommorow and the day after (see *box*).

A GRASSROOTS 'ECO-FEMINISM'

The response of women in an Andean village to a proposal by male officials to plant eucalyptus:

in the community of Tapuc . . . women vehemently said in Quechua that the transplanted eucalyptus in the parcels of *manay* must be immediately removed. *Manay* is an agricultural zone dedicated to the cultivation of root crops, in turns dictated by the system of sectoral flows, with years of rest in between. The community and individuals of the community exercise control together over the *manay*. Thus, the women, speaking for the community, insisted that these parcels had been inherited from their grandparents to supply root crops, they were not going to feed their children with the eucalyptus leaves. Moreover, where the eucalyptus grows, the soil is impoverished and it does not even grow onions.

Source: Enrique Mayer and Cesar Fonseca, *Comunidad y Producion en el Peru* (Lima 1988), p. 187 (translated by Juan Martinez Alier).

AN INDIA/BRAZIL COMPARISON

I move on now to a comparison of the environmental movement as it has unfolded in two large, complex and vitally important Third World countries. Brazil and India have much in common: their sheer size in geographical and demographic terms; the cultural diversity of their societies; the deep disparities between rich and poor; the history of ambitious and aggressive programs of state-sponsored industrialization; the appalling ecological and social costs of these programs; and last, the emergence of active environmental constituencies which have challenged the prevailing consensus on what constitutes proper development.

After World War II, politicians in both Brazil and India were in the vanguard of the movement among the poorer nations of the globe that sought to accomplish in a generation what had taken the affluent West centuries to achieve. The intelligentsia—scientists, technologists, civil servants, legislators—manifested an enormous sense of self-importance, viewing themselves as a chosen elite, leading their people out of darkness into light, or from disease-ridden poverty to prosperity. Pride of place was given to mammoth and pharaonic projects—steel mills, big dams, nuclear power plants and the like—which, it was hoped, would generate wealth and instil a sense of pride and self-worth among the public at large. These projects had their costs—thousands of people displaced, millions of hectares of forests felled and dozens of rivers fouled—but they were at first insulated from criticism by the prestige they enjoyed, the promise they held, and above all by the fact that they were initiated by a government which enjoyed a fair degree of popular support. Projects were legitimated by the ideal of national 'sacrifice:' when tribals had to hand over their forest to a paper mill, for example, or when peasants had to flee from the rising waters of a reservoir designed to inundate their lands, they were offered the solace that this often unwilling sacrifice of their livelihood was being made for the greater good of the nation, or more precisely for the happy augmentation of its Gross National Product.

In both the Brazilian and Indian models of development, the public sector was mandated to control the 'commanding heights' of the economy, with private capitalists assigned an important subsidiary role in generating wealth. Both public and private firms were, however, allowed the virtually free use of nature and natural resources: the state providing them timber, water, minerals, electricity, etc. at well below market prices, and also granting them what was, in effect, the right to freely pollute the air and the waters.

In Brazil the process of industrialization was perhaps more callous than in India. For one thing, the youthfulness of the national culture and the existence of an 'untapped frontier' in the form of the Amazon basin prompted a greater optimism about development and an acceleration of the pace at which it was to be carried out. For another, the country lacked a tradition of dissent such as Gandhism, which in India provided a cautionary voice to temper the impatience of the planners and developers, forcing them to make haste slowly and to take more account of the human costs involved. A vibrant multi-party system and multi-lingual press also gave freer play in India to a variety of voices. In Brazil, by contrast, an already fragile polity was captured in 1964 by a military dictatorship that simply wouldn't tolerate opposition to the highways it built or the licenses it gave on generous terms to industrial firms.

By the late sixties, however, the failures of state-sponsored in-dustrialization lay exposed in both countries. Poverty refused to go away, the fruits of development, such as they were, being garnered by a minority of affluent urbanites and rural landlords. The latter drove cars, watched television, and used refrigerators like their North-ern counterparts, while the majority of their countrymen and women continued to live in huts and shanty towns, cooking their meals with fuelwood or kerosene and relying on their own two feet for locomo-tion. At the same time, nature lay embattled and scarred, subject to levels of environmental degradation that were, in a word, horrific. The social and ecological costs are summed up in the following quotes, both pertaining to Brazil, but both equally true of India. First, some remarks of the sociologist Peter Berger, from his 1974 book *Pyra-mids of Sacrifice*:

> The overall picture that emerges is that of two nations, one relatively affluent, the other in various degrees of misery. Such a state of affairs, of course, exists in many countries of the Third World. The sheer size of Brazil, however, with its enormous territory and its population of about one hundred million, makes for a particular situation. Using reasonable criteria of differentiation, one may divide this population into about fifteen million in the sector of affluence and eighty-five million in the sector of misery. To see the economic import of these figures, one must focus on the fact that fifteen million is a very large number of people—indeed, it is the population of quite a few important countries with advanced industrial economies. As one commentator put it, Brazil is a Sweden superimposed upon an Indonesia. . . . In this way, the very size of Brazil contributes an additional dimension to the process of polarization. It also contributes a seeming plausibility to the rhetoric of the regime. With a little luck, a visitor may travel all over the country and see nothing but 'Sweden,' with some bits of 'Indonesia' either being absorbed into the former or serving as a colorful backdrop for it.
>
> This is the dry stuff of economics. Behind it lies a world of human pain. For a very large segment of the population, life continues to be a

grim struggle for physical survival . . . Millions of people in Brazil are severely undernourished, and some are literally starving to death. Millions of people in Brazil are afflicted with diseases directly related to malnutrition and lack of elementary public hygiene . . . It is on these realities that one must focus in relation to the economic data on unemployment, income distribution, and so on. The crucial fact is: These are realities that kill human beings.

Berger wrote at a time when environmental awareness was not a hallmark of the discipline of sociology; thus his diagnosis, accurate on its own terms, should be supplemented by these later observations of the ecologist Eduardo Viola:

Uncontrolled exploitation of the forests and irrational monoculture are transforming important areas of the south, southeast, centre-west and Amazonic region into deserts . . . The debris of industrial production, the residues of toxics used in agriculture and the sewage dumped directly into rivers, have seriously endangered water resources. The quality of public water supplies consumed in the greater part of Brazil is dreadful when measured against internationally accepted standards. Industrial gases . . . have turned the atmosphere of Brazilian industrial cities into multipliers and generators of respiratory diseases. Cars produced in Brazil, with the exception of those made for export, are not installed with antipollution devices . . . On top of this, the general absence of sewers and inadequate treatment of refuse (aided and abetted by irresponsible sectors of the population who throw their rubbish anywhere, and also by public departments who rarely make provision for means of proper disposal and processing) transform cities into true 'minefields' from the point of public health. . . . Finally, to crown socio-environmental degradation, the production of arms takes up a significant part of the industrial and scientific-technological effort of the country, making Brazil the fifth exporter of arms in the world league.

That ungainly term, socioenvironmental degradation, emphasizes how this litany of natural abuse, which could have come straight out of an Indian environmentalist tract, is as much a human as an 'ecological' disaster. The felling of forests destroys soils and biodiversity, but also throws gatherers and collectors out of work. Toxics kill fish and radically alter the p.h. count of rivers, but simultaneously expose communities to health hazards by contaminating their sole source of drinking water. Car emissions help make Sao Paulo and New Delhi among the ten most polluted cities in the world, but also further debilitate the ill-nourished among urban dwellers. However, this process operates differentially among social classes, for the rich are better insulated from the environmental degradation they cause, enjoy easier access to clean air and water, and can more easily move away from or withstand pollution.

At the first major United Nations environmental conference held in Stockholm in 1972, the governments of India and Brazil were vocal in their defense of development over environment. The Indian prime minister, Mrs Indira Gandhi, delivered a stirring speech to the effect that if pollution was the price of progress, her people wanted more of it; the Brazilian representatives hinted, in the same vein, at the conference being a sinister conspiracy to prevent the developing world from developing further. Whether these official voices accurately represented the views of citizens was already a moot question. A year before Stockholm, a group of professionals led by the respected agronomist José Lutzemberger had founded the Gaucho Association for the Protection of the Natural Environment, or AGAPAN. This is generally held to be the first important environmental initiative in Brazil, the direct analogue of India's Chipko or hug-the-tree movement, which began a year after that first U.N. conference.

In the decades since the founding of AGAPAN and Chipko, environmentalism in both nations has emerged as a genuinely popular movement, country-wide in its reach, and taking up a range of ecological and social concerns. Environmental struggles in Brazil and India have revolved around a shared set of issues: forests, dams, pollution, biodiversity. This is no 'elitist' environmentalism but a movement that has taken into its fold communities at the bottom of the heap. In Brazil the environmentalism of the poor emanates from urban squatters and indigenous people responding to swift and dramatic degradation (such as pollution and the burning of forests), whereas in India it has been the preserve of long-settled rural communities—farmers, fisherfolk, pastoralists, and swidden cultivators—responding to the takeover by the state or by private companies of the common property resources they depend on (see *box*). In both countries protesters have tended to take the militant route, preferring methods of direct action to the patient petitioning of government officials and the judiciary. Brazilian and Indian greens have both been supported by sympathetic coverage in the media. The movements are also united in what they neglect: most strikingly, the role of population growth in fuelling environmental degradation. Catholics in Brazil are temperamentally disinclined to talk of birth control; Gandhians in India dismiss talk of 'over-population' as 'Neo-Malthusianism;' both groups train their guns on social inequities, in their view more centrally responsible for the deterioration of the environment.

RENEWING THE LAND, AND THE
PEOPLE TOO

In 1985 sixty scholars, journalists and social workers issued a
'Statement of Shared Concern on the State of India's
Environment.' Excerpts:

The process of transforming India into a wasteland, which began under the British rule, has continued under post-independence governments. The most brutal assault has been on the country's common property resources, on its grazing lands, forests, rivers, ponds, lakes, coastal zones and increasingly on the atmosphere. The use of these common property resources has been organised and encouraged by the state in a manner that has led to their relentless degradation and destruction. . . .

Nature can never be managed well unless the people closest to it are involved in its management. . . . Common natural resources were earlier regulated through diverse, decentralized, community-control systems. But the state's policy of converting common property resources into government property resources has put them under the control of centralized bureaucracies, who in turn had put them at the service of the more powerful. Today, with no participation of the common people in the management of local resources, even the poor have become so marginalised and alienated from their environment that they are ready to discount their future and sell away the remaining natural resources for a pittance.

Indian villages have traditionally been integrated agrosylvopastoral entities, with grazing lands, agricultural fields, forests and groves, and water sources like ponds, wells and tanks. The state's development programmes have torn asunder this integrated character of the villages. . . .

The process of state control over natural resources that started with the period of colonialism must be rolled back. The earlier community control systems . . . were often unjust and needed restructuring. Given the changed socio-economic circumstances and greater pressure on natural resources, new community control systems have to be established that are more highly integrated, scientifically sophisticated, equitable and sustainable. This is the biggest challenge before India's political system— not just the politicians and their parties, but also citizens and social activists. . . . India can beat the problem of poverty, unemployment, drudgery and oppression only if the country learns to manage its natural resource base in an equitable and ecologically sound way. . . .

Source: *India: the State of the Environment 1984–85: the Second Citizens' Report* (New Delhi: Centre for Science and Environment, 1985), pp. 394–7.

Brazil differs from India in at least three major ways, all of which are reflected in the manner in which its environmental movement has at times followed a somewhat divergent path. First, a much higher proportion of its population is based in the cities, where the living conditions—that is, the quality of housing, water, air, and sanitation—vary enormously from locality to locality. The struggle for a better environment in the shanty-towns of Sao Paulo, Rio and the like has been an important feature of the Brazilian green movement. But India is in demographic and cultural terms a more rural-oriented culture. It was Mahatma Gandhi who famously remarked that 'India lives in its villages.' Since most of his followers have followed him in turning their backs to the city, the problems of urban pollution and housing remain low on the environmental agenda. Indian greens have been more comfortable in the forest and countryside, working with peasants plagued by waterlogged soils or with tribals thrown out of their ancestral forest.

A second difference stems from the higher levels of literacy and education in Brazil. In the early seventies, while the military was still in power, the educated middle-class—scientists, lawyers, journalists, etc.—cautiously began advancing an environmental agenda, at first taking up relatively uncontentious issues such as pollution and the protection of green areas. The organization AGAPAN was in the forefront here; it was only with the withdrawal of the military in the late '80s that greens began to more directly challenge the 'system.' In India, on the other hand, environmentalism drew abudantly on traditions of peasant protest; in fact, it was these protests which first alerted the intelligentsia to the problems of forest loss, soil erosion and water depletion. One might say that in India the professional middle-class has been *reactive*, responding slowly and at times unwillingly to the environmentalism of peasants and tribals; whereas in Brazil it has been *proactive*, well-placed to collaborate with and publicize movements of the urban poor as well as of forest-dwellers and dam-displaced people.

Finally, it seems that Brazilian environmentalism has been more deeply influenced by Northern debates. While *Silent Spring* was translated into Portuguese the year it was first printed in English, trans-national bodies such as the International Union for the Conservation of Nature and Natural Resources have also had active and influential Brazilian chapters. American environmentalists, and to some extent the American public as well, have closely followed Brazilian developments and at times tried to influence them. Ecologically speaking, the destruction of the great Amazonian rainforest by settler agriculture and industrial mining has direct implications for life in the

North—through the loss of biodiversity and a sink to absorb carbon emissions—while, on the social side, the plight of indigenous people has played powerfully on the conscience of those whose forefathers ages ago decimated the native inhabitants of North America. Brazilian environmental problems thus have a high international visibility; further encouraged by the proximity—cultural, political and geographical—of the country to the United States of America.

In India, by contrast, neither Northern green classics nor Northern green bodies have had much of a presence. Again, the repercussions of environmental degradation—grave as they are—are contained largely within India, as are the agents of degradation, who are overwhelmingly government departments and private capitalists. In Brazil, however, both foreign firms and foreign aid agencies such as the World Bank have had a determining influence on the process of development through destruction.

These distinctions matter, but in the final reckoning it is the elements common to Brazil and Indian environmentalism that might matter more. In both countries the environmental movement has centrally contributed to a deepening of democracy, working toward a greater openness of decision making and a greater accountability for decision-makers. As José Lutzemberger put it in 1978, 'The citizen is realizing that he needs to participate in politics because if not the bureaucrats [and, I would add, the politicians] will steamroll right over him. He needs to participate to know what is happening and he needs to shout, even if it is in vain.' In both countries the environmental movement has moved beyond a concern with 'quality of life issues' to more directly challenging the official version of what constitutes welfare and prosperity. The politicians still urge citizens to make the necessary sacrifices for 'development;' the greens expose these claims for what they are, that is, as contributing to the persistence of social strife and ecological deterioration. Brazilian greens characterize development as it has unfolded in their country as 'predatory development;' their Indian counterparts replace 'predatory' with 'destructive,' but the meaning remains much the same.

A CHIPKO/CHICO COMPARISON

On March 27, 1973, in a remote Himalayan village high up in the upper Gangetic valley, a group of peasants stopped a group of loggers from felling a stand of hornbeam trees. The trees stood on land owned by the state forest department, which had auctioned them to a sports-goods company in distant Allahabad, on whose behalf the loggers had come. The peasants of Mandal—the name of the village which adjoined the forest patch—prevented felling by threatening to hug or 'stick' to (*Chipko*) the trees. The Mandal episode sparked a series of similar protests through the '70s, a dozen or more episodes whereby hill peasants stopped contractors from felling trees for external markets. These protests collectively constitute the Chipko movement, recognized as one of the most famous environmental initiatives of our times.

Chipko was representative of a wide spectrum of natural-resource conflicts that erupted in different parts of India in the 1970s and 1980s: conflicts over access to forests, fish and grazing resources; conflicts over the effects of industrial pollution and mining; and conflicts over the siting of large dams. One can understand each of these conflicts sequentially, as an unfolding of the processes of *Degradation—Shortages—Protest—Controversy (local)—Controversy (national)*. Applying this scheme to Chipko, for instance, we note that deforestation in the hills led on the one hand to shortages of fuel, fodder and small timber for local communities and on the other to shortages of raw material for wood-based industry (with Himalayan timber being especially prized as the only source of softwood in India). When the state inclined markedly in favor of one party to the conflict, namely industry, the other party, i.e. peasants, responded through collective action. Picked up by a press that is amongst the most voluble in the world, the protests then gave shape to a debate on how best the Himalayan forests should be managed—by communities, the state, or private capital; on what species should be planted and protected—conifers, broad-leaved, or exotics; and on what should constitute the forest's primary product—wood for industry, biomass for villagers, or soil, water and clean air for the community at large. Finally, this region-specific debate led in turn to a national debate on the direction of forest policy in the country as a whole.

Within India there have been numerous little Chipkos, so to speak, but in the broader global context this movement of Himalayan peasants is best compared to the campaign in the Brazilian Amazon associated with the name of Francisco 'Chico' Mendes. Chico Mendes was a labor organizer who achieved international fame for promoting the 'ecology of justice' in a region devastated by reckless economic exploitation. In the Amazon, a massive expansion of the road network—with some 8000 miles built between 1960 and 1984—opened the way for settlers from the south in search of quick fortunes. Roads brought in colonists and took away the timber of mahogany, rosewood, and other valuable trees. In thirty years almost 10 per cent of the territory, a staggering 60 million hectares of forest, or an area larger than France, had been logged or burnt over. An estimated 85 per cent of this had been converted into pastures for livestock; a most inappropriate form of land use on poor soils that were to be exposed and further impoverished by the next downpour of rain. All in all, this has been a colossal ecological disaster: in the words of one Brazilian scholar, 'the burning of the Amazonian forests represents the most intensive destruction of biomass in world history.'

Among the human communities affected by this devastation were collectors and harvesters of forest produce such as rubber, Brazil nuts, and the babasso palm. Unfortunately, these people often did not have firm legal titles to the land and forests they worked, whereas the ranchers and loggers had on their side the powers of a government determined to exploit and rapidly 'develop' the region. When the forests were taken over by ranchers—sometimes at gun-point—they lost their lands as well as their livelihoods. In the province of Acre, for example, ranchers bought 6 million hectares between 1970 and 1975, in the process displacing more than 10,000 rubber tappers. Aided by men such as Mendes, the tappers resorted to their own innovative form of protest: the *empaté* or stand-off. Men, women and children marched to the forest, joined hands, and dared the workers and their chain-saws from proceeding further. The first *empaté* took place on March 10, 1976—three years after the first Chipko protest. Over the next decade, a series of stand-offs helped save two million acres of forest from conversion into pastureland.

From the mid 1970s the rubber tappers have had a vigorous union of their own, and in 1987 they joined hands with the indigenous inhabitants of the Amazon to form a Forest Peoples' Alliance (see *box*). This alliance pledged to defend the forest and land rights of its members. It also worked for the creation of 'extractive reserves,' areas protected from the chain-saw where rubber tappers and others could sustainably harvest what they needed without affecting the forest's capacity for regenerating itself. But as the rubber tappers became more organized, 'the ranchers became more determined in their efforts to drive them off the land,' forming a coalition of their own, the Uniao Democratica Rural. In a region already scarred by high levels of violence, the conflict escalated in tragic ways. In 1980 ranchers and their agents had assassinated Wilson Pinheiro, a prominent union organizer. Eight years later, on December 22, 1988, they finally eliminated Chico Mendes, shot dead as he came out of his house.

There are striking similarities between the Chipko movement and the struggle of Chico Mendes and his associates. Both drew on a long history of peasant resistance to the state and outsiders: in the Himalayan case, stretching back a hundred years and more. Both thought up novel and nonviolent forms of protest to stop tree-felling; protest forms in which women constituted the front-line of defense, a tactical move that worked well in inhibiting loggers. In each case the leadership was provided not by city-bred or educated activists but by 'organic' intellectuals from *within* the community. Neither struggle was merely content with asking the loggers to go home: the Forest Peoples Alliance proposed sustainable reserves, whereas Chipko workers have successfully mobilized peasant women in protecting and replenishing their village forests. Both movements have

---

AMAZONIAN VOICES

In its second national meeting, held in 1989, the Rubber Tappers Council of Brazil offered its 'homage to all those in the struggle who gave their lives for the principles affirming our regional cultures. Especially we remember our most illustrious comrade Chico Mendes.' The Council then resolved to struggle for the following program:

POLICIES FOR DEVELOPMENT FOR
FOREST PEOPLES

1. Models of development that respect the way of life, cultures and traditions of forest peoples without destroying nature, and that improve the quality of life.

2. The right to participate in the process of public discussion of all the government projects for forests inhabited by Indians and rubber tappers as well as other extractive populations, through the associations and entities that represent these workers.

3. Public guarantees to scrutinize and curb the disastrous impacts of projects already destined for Amazonia, and the immediate halt of projects that damage the environment and Amazonian peoples.

4. Information on policies and projects for Amazonia and any large projects to be subject to discussion in Congress, with the participation of the organizations that represent those people affected by these projects.

Based on these principles, the Council also outlined specific programs for agrarian reform, education and health, credit and marketing, and the protection of human rights.

Source: Susanna Hecht and Alexander Cockburn, *The Fate of the Forest: Developers, Destroyers and Defenders of the Amazon* (London: Penguin, 1990), Appendix E.

taken recourse to an ideology that carries wide appeal in their societies. The two best-known Chipko leaders, Chandiprasad Bhatt and Sunderlal Bahuguna, are lifelong Gandhians. Likewise, Catholic priests have supported the rubber-tappers; and as Chico Mendes recalled, when arrested after an *empaté* protesters would sing hymns en route to the police lock-up.

The Chipko movement and Chico Mendes's struggle are broadly comparable but not, of course, identical. While Himalayan deforestation has had disturbing ecological effects—in the shape of increased soil erosion and the incidence of floods—the clearing of the Amazon represents a much more serious loss of biodiversity, through the extinction of hundreds of species of insects, plants, birds and animals. (This is one reason why the Brazilian movement has attracted greater, and continuing, international attention than did Chipko). On the social side, forest conflicts in the Amazon have been characterized by a much higher level of violence. The traditions of democracy are rather less robust in Brazil than in India, and the expression of protest and dissent more likely there to be met with force. It is significant that while we tend to honor the Chipko movement for its *nonviolent* technique of protest, the Amazon struggle is more often remembered, at least outside Brazil, for the *violent* death of its leader.

One must note, finally, the prolific misrepresentations of both movements by the international media. The Amazon struggle is often reduced to the image of Chico Mendes as a 'green martyr' who died trying to 'save the Amazon' from its destroyers. Likewise, the most popular image of Chipko is of unlettered women 'saving the Himalaya' by threatening to hug the trees. There has arisen a mystique around Chipko and Chico that unfortunately obscures their real and deeper meaning, as struggles in which environmental protection has been inseparable from social justice.

REDEFINING DEVELOPMENT

Feeding on indigenous ideologies of justice—Gandhism, Buddhism or Catholicism—and emboldened by a more general assertion of 'eco-feminism,' the environmentalism of the poor has contributed to a profound rethinking of the idea of development itself. Intellectuals sympathetic to these movements have fashioned a critique of the industrial and urban bias of government policies, urging that it give way to a decentralized, socially aware, environmentally friendly and altogether more *gentle* form of development. These efforts have sometimes drawn explicitly on the ideas of the early environmentalists

Poster of Chico Mendes, leader of the Brazilian rubber-tappers, issued after the assassination of Mendes in December 1988.

SOURCE Susanna Hecht and Alexander Cockburn, The Fate of the Forest *(Verso Books)*

Estes são os membros da UDR no Acre

João Branco

Darli Alves — Aragão — Narciso Mendes — Rubens Branquinho

EXIGIMOS A PUNIÇÃO DA UDR NO ENVOLVIMENTO DO ASSASSINATO DE CHICO MENDES

Comitê Chico Mendes

Poster of April 1989, demanding action against Mendes' alleged killers.

SOURCE *Susanna Hecht and Alexander Cockburn,* The Fate of the Forest *(Verso Books)* discussed in Chapter II. But they have also been enriched by more contemporary thinking in ecology and the social sciences. Development as conventionally understood and practised has been attacked on a philosophical plane, but critics have been forthcoming with nose-to-the ground, sector-specific solutions as well. In the realm of water management, they have offered to large dams the alternative of small dams and/or the revival of traditional methods of irrigation such as tanks and wells. In the realm of forestry, they have asked whether community control of natural forests is not a more just and sustainable option when compared to the handing over of public land on a platter to industrial plantations. In the realm of fisheries, they have deplored the favors shown to trawlers at the expense of countryboats, suggesting that a careful demarcation of ocean waters, restricting the area in which trawlers can operate, might allow freer play to indigenous methods as well as facilitate the renewal of fish stocks.

As in the North then, in the South too there is an active environmental debate as well as environmental movement. To be sure, there are some salient differences to be noted. Where Northern environmentalism has highlighted the significance of value change (the shift to 'postmaterialism'), Southern movements seem to be more strongly rooted in material conflicts, with the claims of economic justice—that is, the rights to natural resources of poorer communities—being an integral part of green movements. This is why these movements work not only for culture change but also, and sometimes more directly, for a change in the production system (see *box*). And where Southern groups have tended to be more adversarial with regard to their government—opposing laws and policies deemed to be destructive or unjust—Northern groups have more often had a constructive side to their programs, working with their governments in promoting environmentally benign laws and policies.

In both contexts there has now accumulated a rich body of reflective work to complement direct action: although in the poorer countries the line of causation seems to run the other way, with intellectual reflection, for the most part, being prompted by or following popular protest (in contrast to the North, where books like *Silent Spring* might even be said to have sparked off the environmental movement). Finally, while Northern greens have been deeply attentive to the rights of victimized or endangered animal and plant species, Southern greens have generally been more alert to the rights of the less fortunate members of their own species.

One thing that brings together environmentalists in both contexts, however, is the anti-environmental lobby they have to contend

ENVIRONMENTALISM AND THE DEEPENING
OF DEMOCRACY
*Henry David Thoreau once remarked that 'In Wildness is the
Preservation of the World.' The experience of modern Brazil seems to call
for a postscript, that 'In Democracy is the Preservation of the
Environment,' as these passages from a recent book explain:*

The struggle against environmental degradation has increasingly come to
be understood as a part of the democratic struggle to build and consolidate
a new model for citizenship. Efforts to promote environmental rights
have brought together numerous segments of the social movement, who
have sought to ensure access to essential public goods such as water and
air in adequate amounts and with sufficient quality to guarantee decent
living standards; the use of collective goods needed for the social
reproduction of specific socio-cultural groups such as rubber tappers,
nut gatherers, fishermen, and indigenous people; a guarantee for the
public use of natural resources such as green areas, waterways, headwaters
and ecosystems, which have often been degraded by private interests that
are incompatible with society's collective concerns. . . .

. . . It [is] clear that in the Brazilian socio-environmental crisis,
ecological degradation and social inequality are two branches stemming
from the same root, namely, the specific ways in which capitalism has
developed in Brazil by throwing peasants off their land, expanding the
frontiers of agri-business, encouraging land speculation and deforestation,
wearing out land and drying up rivers, making traditional fishing and
forest extractivism unfeasible, adopting an environmentally harmful
industrial standard, overloading urban structures, concentrating wealth,
and marginalizing population groups. . . .

. . . It is necessary to seek a kind of development that is not limited
to preserving the supply and prices of natural resources as productive
inputs. The majority of the Brazilian population is not interested in a
kind of development that pretends to be 'sustainable' simply by technically
reconverting productive systems and adopting a capitalist rationale in the
use of natural resources. We should seek to change the determinant logic
of development and make the environmental variable be incorporated as
a component of the people's living and working conditions. This kind of
change only depends secondarily on possibilities for technical progress.
In fact, it depends primarily on the democratization of political
processes. . . . To democratize control over natural resources, to
deprivatize an environment that is common to society and nations, to
introduce democracy into environmental administration, and to ensure
the public character of common natural patrimony constitute the agenda
of issues [for the environmental movement] . . .

Source: Henri Acselrad, editor, *Environment and Democracy*
(Botafogo: IBASE, 1992), Preface.

with. In countries such as the United States, businessmen and industrialists have been the most hostile critics of the greens. In India and
Malaysia they are joined by state officials and technocrats, with both
private and public promoters of development attacking environmentalists as motivated by foreigners, as creating law-and-order problems,
or as wishing only to keep tribals and rural people 'backward,' placed
in a museum for themselves and their fellow romantics to gawk at.
The most famous and powerful of these anti-environmentalists has
been the Prime Minister of Malaysia, Mahathir bin Mohammed. In
1990, he announced that he and his government did not

> intend to turn the Penan into human zoological specimens to be gawked
> at by tourists and studied by anthropologists while the rest of the world
> passes them by . . . It's our policy to eventually bring all jungle dwellers
> into the mainstream . . . There is nothing romantic about these helpless,
> half-starved and disease-ridden people.

Two years later, in a document specially prepared for the Earth Summit, Mahathir's government insisted that

> The transition from cave and forest dwelling to village and urban living
> is a phenomenon that has marked the transformation of human societies
> from time immemorial. The environmental activists have no right to
> stand in the way of the Penans in this process of change and human
> development.

Not only with regard to the Penan, not just in Malaysia, it has been
the signal contributions of environmental activists to speak truth to
power, to ask of politicians and other rulers the uncomfortable questions: Development at what cost? Progress at whose expense?

7

Socialism and Environmentalism (or the Lack Thereof)

EARLY SOVIET ENVIRONMENTALISM

The affluent societies of the Europe and North America, along with Japan, Australia, and New Zealand, are collectively known as the 'First' World; the poorer nations of the South, located in Africa, Asia, and Latin America, as the 'Third' World. This book has highlighted thinkers and movements from the First and Third Worlds, but has thus far left unmentioned the people and territories in between. It now arrives at the Second World, the countries behind the Iron Curtain which are neither rich nor poor and were distinguished, before the fall of the Berlin Wall in 1989, by their commitment to the ideology of state socialism. The discussion shall focus on the Soviet Union, the erstwhile superpower that was the Big Brother of the Second World.

The previous chapter has spoken of the obsession of Brazilian and Indian politicians with catching up with the affluent societies. This obsession in fact manifested itself much earlier in the Soviet Union, soon after the First rather than the Second World War. The leaders of the Bolshevik Revolution of November 1917 hoped to catch up in military as well as economic terms, for they believed that only breakneck industrialization would save their beleaguered country from being overrun by the capitalist powers. As Joseph Stalin once said, 'We are fifty to one hundred years behind the most advanced countries. We must close this gap in the span of ten years. Either we do that or they will sweep us away.' The worship of technology, the faith in industrial production as a means of solving social problems, the arrogant neglect of natural constraints, all helped shade the difference between Soviet communism and American capitalism. Writing in 1933, Aldo Leopold wrote insightfully of what worked to unite political systems apparently opposed to each other:

> As nearly as I can see, all the new isms—Socialism, Communism, Fascism ... outdo even Capitalism itself in their preoccupation with one thing: the distribution of more machine-made commodities to more people. Though they despise each other they are competitive apostles of a single creed: *salvation by machinery*.

Soviet programs of industrial reconstruction were buttressed by Marxism, an ideology which has an unshakeable faith in the powers of modern technology to tame and conquer nature. Marxists also believed that the abolition of private property leads automatically to a diminution of pollution, for the victory of communism would eliminate the capitalists who stoop to anything—putting untreated effluents into the water, for example—to protect their profits. In this view, any residual contamination of the environment would be taken care of by the all-seeing and all-knowing system of centralized planning.

With regard to philosophy and practice, then, Soviet Marxism was characterized, in the main, by a deep indifference to nature and natural limits. 'The proper goal of communism,' remarked Leon Trotsky in the early 1920s, 'is the domination of nature by technology, and the domination of technology by planning, so that the raw materials of nature will yield up to mankind all that it needs and more besides.' A decade later a Soviet scientist claimed that 'the history of humankind has been the road from slavery and blind subjection to the elemental forces of nature to the struggle [and] conquest of her ... In conditions of socialism ... the natural resource base for the economy is not contracting, but has all of the ingredients for limitless development.'

The signs were unpropitious, but as it happened in the first ten years of communist rule a fledgeling conservation movement was to take impressive strides. There already existed a rich pre-revolutionary tradition of natural history and nature protection societies which had helped set aside endangered habitats. In the first week of November 1917, concurrent with the Bolshevik assumption of power, a Conservation Conference in Petrograd discussed a proposal 'On the Types

of Sites where it is Necessary to Establish *Zapovedniki* on the Model
of the American National Parks.' In fact the Russian understanding
of *Zapovedniki*, or protected areas, was more sophisticated than the
American. National Parks in the U.S. had been established for cultural
and nationalist reasons, whereas Soviet scientists were asking for sites
of virgin nature to be selected on *ecological* criteria, to act as a 'baseline'
from which to judge the suitability of human intervention in other,
so to say unprotected areas.

LEON TROTSKY ON THE
SOCIALIST CONQUEST OF NATURE
*One of the architects of the Russian Revolution outlines his
vision of socialist man's domination of nature.*

The present distribution of mountains and rivers, of fields, of meadows,
of steppes, of forests and seashores, cannot be considered final. Man has
already made changes in the map of nature that are not few nor
insignificant. But they are mere pupil's practice in comparison with what
is coming. Faith merely promises to move mountains; but technology,
which takes nothing 'on faith', is actually able to cut down mountains and
move them. Up to now this was done for industrial purposes (mines) or
for railways (tunnels); in the future this will be done on an immeasurably
larger scale, according to a general industrial and artistic plan. Man will
occupy himself with re-registering mountains and rivers, and will earnestly
and repeatedly make improvements in nature. In the end, he will have re-
built the earth, if not in his own image, at least according to his taste. We
have not the slightest fear that this taste will be bad . . .
 . . . Through the machine, man in socialist society will command nature
in its entirety . . . He will point out places for mountains and passes. He
will change the course of the rivers, and he will lay down rules for the
oceans. The idealist simpletons may say that this will be a bore, but that
is why they are simpletons . . .

Source: Leon Trotsky, quoted in C. Wright Mills, *The Marxists*
(Harmondsworth: Penguin Books, 1963), pp. 278–9.

 Indeed, in the early years of Soviet rule both scientific research
and university education flourished. The historian Douglas Weiner
speaks of the 1920s as 'a golden age' for the teaching of biology in
Russia. No longer subject to the 'shackles of the obscurantist Roma-
nov censors, biology was free to introduce the most advanced notions
into the classroom. An entire generation of geneticists, ecologists,
and experimental biologists of world rank was in formation.'

Some names might be offered here. Among biologists of world repute were N. I. Vavilov, the great student, collector and classifier of crop races; and G. F. Gauze, who pioneered the idea of the 'ecological niche' of a species. One must also mention V. I. Vernadskii, the scholar to whom we owe the terms 'biosphere' and 'geosphere:' it was Vernadskii who, forty years before the publication of the *Limits to Growth* report of the Club of Rome, pointed out that natural productive forces 'have limits and that these limits are real; they are not imaginary and they are not theoretical. They may be ascertained by the scientific study of nature and represent for us an insuperable natural limit to our productive capacity.' A fourth scientist of note was the entomologist A. P. Semenov-tian-shanskii, who combined laboratory expertise with a romantic love of nature. Semenov-tian-shanskii was to will his collection of 700,000 insects to the Zoological Museum in Moscow; this included specimens of 900 species which he had discovered and first described himself. Little wonder that he thought nature to be the 'great book of the existence of all things,' a museum 'indispensable for our further enlightenment and mental development, a museum which, in the event of its destruction, cannot be reconstructed by the hand of man.' Society, believed Semenov-tian-shanskii, had 'a great moral obligation toward Nature,' yet industrial man was showing himself to be a 'geological parvenu . . . disrupting the harmony of nature,' determined to destroy 'that grand tableau which serves as the inspiration of the arts.'

This efflorescence of scientific research was accompanied by the creation and consolidation of conservation societies. These included the Central Bureau for the Study of Local Lore (TsBK, in its Russian acronym), which worked for the protection of natural as well as cultural heritage; a regional body, the All-Ukranian Society for the Defense of Animals and Plants (ZhIVRAS); and the All-Russian Society for Conservation (VOOP), which drew into its fold some of the most distinguished Soviet scientists. By the late twenties TsBK boasted of 2000 branches and 60,000 members; the Ukranian society claimed a membership of 9000; VOOP had only 1400 paid-up members, but it brought out the influential journal *Okhrana prirody*, an illustrated bi-monthly with a circulation in excess of 3000.

Scientists and their societies were encouraged by the Soviet dictator Vladimir Illyich Lenin, who was the brother of a biologist and a trekker and nature lover himself. It was Lenin who signed, in September 1921, a new decree for the 'Protection of Monuments of Nature, Gardens and Parks,' which prohibited hunting and fishing in existing *zapovedniki* and encouraged the establishment of new ones. By 1929 there were 61 *zapovedniki* in the USSR, covering an area close to 4 million hectares. Woods falling outside these protected areas were governed by a Forest Code which was signed into law in July 1923: this promoted reforestation and sustained-yield logging while prohibiting clear-cutting in districts where forest cover was less than 8 per cent of the land area.

In retrospect the 1920s appear to have been a golden age for Soviet science and for Soviet environmentalism as well. 'Ecological conservation's moment in the Soviet sun,' remarks Weiner ruefully, 'was tragically brief.' There seem to be uncanny parallels between the defeat of Gandhism in India and the retreat of environmentalism in the USSR. Both streams, after promising beginnings, were vanquished by the rise to power of a philosophy of state-led industrialization that would not recognize natural constraints. But where the Gandhians merely went back to their *ashrams*, their Russian counterparts were less fortunate. Vernadskii, for example, spent many years in exile; Gauze was prohibited from designing new experiments; most tragic of all was the end of Vavilov, who, having crossed swords with the impostor Trofim Lysenko—Stalin's pet biologist—died in prison.

The demise of Soviet environmentalism was signalled by the first Five-Year Plan of 1929–34, which sought to radically alter production methods in agriculture and industry. The plan mandated an increase in timber production from 178 to 280 million cubic metres; other targets were equally far-reaching. There was now relentless pressure on ecologists to show 'results,' to make their research lead directly to the economic exploitation of natural resources. The collectivization of agriculture destroyed numerous protected areas on the steppes, converting natural biological communities into fields. Mining and logging were allowed in other wild areas. Where *zapovedniki* once covered 12.5 million hectares, by the early '50s this had declined to a mere 1.5 million hectares.

Ecologists and conservationists were on the defensive, in a professional as much as psychological sense. The attacks on them and their work were unforgiving. Commissars and communists thundered that there was no place any more for a 'saccharine-sentimental' approach to nature, for the 'naked idea of preservationism' which had, they thought, inhibited the further development of socialism. The TsBK was mocked as a 'Society for the Preservation of Antiquity,' a 'Society for Protection *from* the Revolution.' Scientific societies were compared to *zapovedniki* where protected professors roamed. The aim of the societies, it was said, was to 'save nature from the Five-Year Plan.' Respected scholars known for their conservationist views were dismissed as un-Marxist or anti-revolutionary, even as 'agents of the world bourgeoisie.'

Soviet conservation in its first and most fruitful phase had room for three distinct varieties of environmentalism: for ecologists who favored the protection of undisturbed wilderness; for those who combined careful science with rural romanticism; and for practitioners of sustained-yield management. By the late '30s the first two orientations had disappeared into near-oblivion. The third strand, of scientific conservation, still existed, but in an uneasy coalition with state-planned industrialization. A scientist who found himself on the winning side wrote that it was

> evident that the old theory of conservation of nature for nature's sake—
> a proposition that reeks of ancient cults of Nature's deification—stands
> in such sharp opposition to both our economic and our scientific interests
> that there is no place for it in our land of socialism-in-the-making ... Not
> the preservation, come what may, of the existing state of nature, but the
> rational intervention, study, mastery, and regulation of natural productive
> forces—that is what should be emblazoned on the banners of our society.

When assessing the fate of Soviet environmentalism, the political climate in which it lived and died must never be overlooked. For the Russia of the 1930s and 1940s was the most totalitarian of societies, a place in which intellectual or political dissent was impermissible. N. I. Vavilov was one of an estimated 1,500,000 scholars, writers and revolutionaries who perished in the death camps for putting forward, however mildly, opinions that departed from the party line. Quite aside from the pressures of economics, then, there were very real constraints to the expression of environmentalist views that lay outside the narrow range of what was considered acceptable in Soviet Russia.

THE THREE GORGES PROJECT: A PROTEST THAT WASN'T

In 1956, the all-powerful Chairman of China's Communist Party took a swim in the great Yangtze river; coming out of the water, he looked forward to more spectacular demonstrations of man's powers over nature:

SWIMMING

by Mao Zedong

Great plans are being made;
A bridge will fly to join the north and south,
A deep chasm will become a thoroughfare;
Walls of stone will stand upstream to the west
To hold back Wushan's clouds and rain,
Till a smooth lake rises in the narrow gorges.
The mountain goddess, if she is still there
Will marvel at a world so changed.

[translated by John Gittings]

Great plans had first been made, in fact, in the 1920s, when the nationalist leader Sun Yat-Sen suggested the building of a dam across the Three Gorges, on the river's upper reaches. The idea was revived by Mao in the '50s, but it took another thirty years for it to move from the politician's poems to the engineer's sketches. As now proposed by China's planners, the Three Gorges Dam will be 185 metres (620 feet) high, generate 17,000 megawatts of electricity, take twenty years to build, and cost a staggering 50 billion U.S. dollars (224 billion yuan). It will be a feat of 'engineering giganticism,' the last defiant symbol of state planning, the last of the heroic projects, comparable in the country's history only to the Great Wall itself.

Communist China treats dissent with the same arrogance as did Soviet Russia, but in early 1989 a group of brave journalists and scholars came together to publish a book, *Yangtze! Yangtze!*, which took a cold and critical look at the Three Gorges project. Printed in February, the book was at first widely and sympathetically covered in the media. It formed part of the 'Peking Thaw,' the wider pro-democracy movement that reached its peak with the students' peaceful capture of the city's Tiannenmen Square. After the military fired on the demonstrators in June, the movement collapsed, and the state came down heavily on the opponents of the dam. Several were jailed; *Yangtze! Yangtze!* was banned soon after the bloodbath, its remaining copies recalled from stores and pulped.

The contributors to *Yangtze! Yangtze!* included some of China's most respected hydrologists, physicists, ecologists and planners. Their criticisms of the Three Gorges project focused on its techno-economic unviability. These scientists argued that the massive borrowing of funds would generate unacceptably high levels of inflation; that the project's promoters had grossly over-estimated benefits and under-estimated costs; that the dam would not help control floods; that it would seriously impede ship traffic on the Yangtze, which presently carried goods and passengers equivalent to fourteen railway lines; that it would increase sedimentation, leading to the decline of an important port, Chongquing; and that it would direct funds away from small-scale projects that were more practicable, less destructive and would produce quicker results.

These technical criticisms were accompanied by social, environmental and aesthetic ones. The dam would, when built, displace as many as 1.3 million people. Yet, as one scholar pointed out, for this 'massive population relocation' the planners offered a 'resettlement plan [which] is ridiculous.' The region, noted another expert, is 'already an overpopulated area where food is insufficient and the land depleted. To resettle a population as large as that of a small European country will certainly exceed the local environmental capacity of this mountainous region.' Most eloquent of all was the lament of the veteran botanist Hou Xueyu:

> Apart from irreparable damage to the soil, the natural beauty and cultural heritage of the area would be permanently damaged as well. I think the Three Gorges is the most beautiful of all the world's gorges. The surrounding areas have many national treasures, some more than 5,000 years old. These include the famous ruins of the ancient Daxi culture, and tombs from the Warring States period, the Eastern Han and the Ming and Qing dynasties . . . Further, the Three Gorges has unique geological features that provide very important physical data for research. All this would be inundated if the reservoir were built, and tourism would suffer incalculable economic losses.

All over the world, large dams are being challenged as 'outdated monuments to an immodest era,' symbols of a centralizing, capital-intensive and environment-insensitive form of development that is no longer acceptable. The Chinese critics of the Three Gorges project are aware of, and take heart from, this world-wide movement. They grimly note that the construction of the Itaipu hydro-electric project—the grandest anywhere—was one of several such schemes that massively increased the Brazilian public debt, leading to an inflation rate of 365 per cent. They look hopefully across at the Silent Valley in south India and at the Franklin river in Australia, two instances where projected dams were called off after popular protest.

Tragically, the prospects of open and collective protest in China are close to zero. Elsewhere, in Brazil and India for example, people threatened with displacement have organized large processions, defiantly uprooted reservoir markers, marched on provincial and national capitals and burnt effigies of offending politicians and technocrats. These protests have not always been successful in stopping the dam; but at least they happen. In China, on the other hand, the million and more victims of the Three Gorges project must silently suffer as it is being built: criticisms being offered only by courageous scientists who were themselves swiftly silenced. In April 1992, a committee of the Communist Party finally voted to give the go-ahead to the dam. The next January, a Three Gorges Project Development Corporation was set up to oversee construction. An array of foreign firms, including Nippon and Merril Lynch, lined up to bid for contracts.

The conflict between environmental protection and authoritarian rule can only sharpen in China, a country which has liberalized its economic regime while remaining a one-party state. The industrial boom of the last decade has generated enormous amounts of pollution, but citizens are gravely inhibited from doing anything about it. In August 1993, villagers in Gansu Province protested against the contamination of their water by a chemical plant, leading to deaths of fish and livestock and an increase in respiratory illnesses. When the factory's managers, themselves well connected to the Communist Party, disregarded their complaints, peasants took to the streets. Riot police were called in; they killed two protesters and injured several others before restoring 'order.'

The Chinese government, indeed, will not even permit the formation of a non-political group of nature-lovers. A celebrated historian, Lian Congjie, applied in 1993 to register a society to be called the 'Friends of Nature,' which would 'work to educate China's populace about the importance of environmental conservation.' Permission was not refused but was not granted either, the application being ignored by officials. The editor of *Yangtze! Yangtze!*, Dai Qing, notes that 'even though Liang Congjie says "I'm not interested in politics; I only want to help the environment," the government doesn't believe him.'

DEMOCRACY AND ENVIRONMENTALISM, AND THE TIES THAT BIND THEM

The president of the Chinese Banking Association, Qiao Peixin, remarked that in the 'debate over the Three Gorges project, I am afraid that there has not been enough democracy; the affirmative voices are allowed to be heard but the negative voices are often suppressed.' The woman journalist who edited *Yangtze! Yangtze!* likewise observed, after the book was banned, that

Today, many Chinese and foreign newspapers and magazines have labeled me an 'environmentalist.' I am quite flattered by the title. Although I have a great deal of respect for the environmental movement, neither I nor my colleagues considered ourselves environmentalists when we were compiling and publishing *Yangtze! Yangtze!* Our goal was to push China a little bit further towards freedom of speech on the issue of government decision making.

The ideology of state socialism is antithetical to environmentalism on a number of grounds: in its worship of technology; in its arrogant desire to conquer nature; through its system of central planning in which pollution control comes in the way of the fulfilment of production targets. Most of all, though, state socialism has inhibited environmentalism by throttling democracy, by denying to those it rules over the basic freedoms of association, combination, and expression.

DARING TO HOPE, HOPING TO DARE

From an untitled poem by Bei Dao, translated by Geremie Barmé, and quoted at the very end of a book that presented the case against the mammoth Three Gorges dam project:

I do not believe that the Chinese will forever
    refuse to think for themselves;
I do not believe that the Chinese will never
    speak out through their writings;
I do not believe that morality and justice will
    vanish in the face of repression;
I do not believe that in an age in which
    we are in communication with the world,
'freedom of speech' will remain an empty phrase.

Source: Dai Qing, editor, *Yangtze! Yangtze!* (English edition: London: Earthscan, 1994), p. 265.

If in China protests against the Three Gorges dam surfaced in the brief thaw of 1988–89, elsewhere in the communist world environmental movements came to form part of a wider struggle for democracy. In Poland, where the trade union Solidarity led the opposition to Communism, it was also Solidarity which, through its local chapters, began studying and publicizing incidents of environmental abuse. All over Eastern Europe, as the struggle against totalitarianism gathered force in the 1980s, environmental groups began holding the state to account for its 'crimes against nature.' These crimes spoke for themselves: that in Poland the contamination of the environment had reduced life expectancy between 1970 and 1985; that in Czechoslovakia more than 50 per cent of the forest area had been damaged by acid rain; that in Romania an independent study identified a massive 625 centers of serious pollution; that in Russia the great Lake Baikal was dying a slow and painful death due to eutrophication.

Previously there had been little opportunity to speak out against all this, a state of affairs remedied by the rise to power, in 1985, of the Soviet leader Mikhail Gorbachev. Gorbachev's policies of *glasnost*, openness, quickly spilled over from the Soviet Union to its satelite states. People were now allowed to breathe more freely, indeed to demand cleaner air. The impetus for the new environmentalism came from a variety of sources: from Solidarity and the Catholic Church in Poland; from evangelical clergy in East Germany; from scientists in Hungary and Czechoslovakia; from plain old-fashioned democrats in Bulgaria and Rumania—home, respectively, to Todor Zhivkov and Nikolai Ceuceascu, the most tyrannical of the Communist tyrants. In these countries environmentalists played a not unimportant role in the revolutions of 1989 that consigned one-party states to oblivion. In the elections which followed, Green parties found parliamentary representation in Rumania, Bulgaria and Slovenia, while in Czechoslovakia environmentalists allied themselves to the victorious Civic Forum led by the green-minded playwright, Vaclav Havel.

In his own land Gorbachev's agenda also resonated nicely with an environmental constituency that had been making itself visible from about a decade before his arrival. One might speak here of two waves of Soviet environmentalism, interrupted of course by a long period of totalitarian rule. Although Joseph Stalin died in 1953 and his 'personality cult' was dramatically disavowed three years later, it took another twenty years for environmentalist writings to start finding a place in the newspapers and literary magazines. But from the mid '70s writers and scientists began gently criticizing the foul-smelling residues of unchecked industrialization. These criticisms became more strident in the mid '80s, following Gorbachev's ascent to power and the near-simultaneous accident at the Chernobyl nuclear plant, this the biggest disaster in a disaster-ridden history of 'planned' development. Numerous groups and societies began banding together— one such was the Ecology and Peace Association, whose President, S. P. Zalygin, offered the stirring motto, 'Only the Public can save Nature.' This public now bestirred itself to save beloved and beleaguered water bodies: which included the rivers Volga and Don, eyed by destructive dam-builders, and Lake Baikal, choked by the effluents of one of the world's biggest paper mills. Away from the great rivers and lakes, citizens came together to challenge polluting industries, forcing them to pay fines, to change over to cleaner processes, or to shut down altogether. By accident or design, many of the more dangerous factories had been sited outside Russia, in the subordinated republics of Estonia, Armenia, and Latvia. Here environmentalists allied themselves to nationalists, associating the offending factories with a Greater Russian Chauvinism, which they accused of craftily exporting polluting units to non-Russian areas.

But as Ze'ev Wolfson points out, this 'marriage of ecology and national history' has also been characteristic of 'a portion of Russia's [own] green movement.' Where Soviet novelists had once extolled steel mills and collective farms, there came to prominence, in the '70s and '80s, a school of writers which looked back lovingly to the peasants of the pre-revolutionary past. The best-known of these 'village' novelists, Valentin Rasputin, wrote a famous fictional defense of a rural community made to make way for a hydro-electric project. He also wrote feelingly of the threatened landscapes of his native Siberia and of Lake Baikal, near whose shores he lived. For Rasputin, as for his contemporary Vasiliy Belov, the village is 'the wellspring of morality, religious meaning, and harmony with the natural environment, and, moreover, the only reliable medium through which these values can be transmitted to future generations.' Or as Yuriy Bondarev put it,

> If we do not stop the destruction of architectural monuments, if we do not stop the violence to the earth and rivers, if there does not take place a moral explosion in science and criticism, then one fine morning, which will be our last and that of our funeral, we, with our inexhaustible optimism, will wake up and realize that the national culture of great Russia—its spirit, its love for the paternal land, its beauty, its great literature, painting, and philosophy—has been effaced, has disappeared forever, murdered, destroyed forever, and we, naked and impoverished, will sit on the ashes, trying to remember the native alphabet which is so dear to our hearts, and we won't be able to remember, for thought, and feeling, and happiness, and historical memory will have disappeared.
>
> [translated from the Russian by Robert G. Darst, Jr.]

This was spoken in 1986 at the annual Congress of the USSR Union of Writers, a body which would not have allowed, in 1966 or in 1946, such a forthright refutation of the economic ideology of communism, an ideology marked by disdain for the past and reverence for the

mighty powers of the modern. But dissent is the life-blood of democracy, and it is not only in communist states that environmentalists
have pushed back the limits of what has been considered politically
acceptable. Thus in the Indonesian island province of Bali, where
militant protests might be met with a hail of bullets, greens who oppose destructive development projects have shrewdly used petitions,
poetry readings, prayers in temples and cartoons in the press. As the
anthropologist Carol Warren remarks, in this one-party state 'environmental issues had become a vehicle for the expression of disaffection
on broader social and political questions.' The connection between
environmental reform and political reform more generally was also
made manifest in a 1990 manifesto of a Bulgarian green organization.
Where the state and party are one, it observed, 'we have privileged
chiefs and unprivileged consumers.' And since 'those who make the
strategic decisions are not the same people as those who have to face
the consequences,' the 'degree of an individual's responsibility in deci-
sion-making is in inverse proportion to the actual suffering caused
[to] him by environmental pollution.'

   This Bulgarian group is called *Ecoglasnost*, a name which bears
testimony to the inseparable link between democracy and environmentalism. For authoritarian states cannot permit the rise of green
movements; conversely green movements might—as in 1970s Brazil
and 1980s Eastern Europe—help move communist or military dic-
tatorships in the direction of multi-party, so to say more open societies. It is no accident that one of the more robust green movements
in the South is to be found in India, a democracy for all but two of its
fifty-two years as an independent republic; or that environmentalism
is most influential in the United States and Western Europe, where
the commitment to political democracy runs deeper than in any other
place or at any other time in human history.

8

One World or Two?

The world's largest conservation organization, the World Wildlife Fund, found a novel way to celebrate its twenty-fifth anniversary in September 1986. It brought together, at the small Italian town of Assisi, representatives of five of the world's great religions—Christianity, Islam, Hinduism, Buddhism and Judaism. Assisi is the birthplace of Saint Francis (1181–1226), the activist friar who was a lover of the poor and of nature, a precociously early environmentalist recognized by a papal bull of 1979 as the 'patron saint' of ecology. Now, some 650 years after his death, a congregation of spiritual leaders gathered at his basilica for a Religion and Nature Inter-Faith Ceremony to 'celebrate the dignity of nature and the duty of every person to live harmoniously within the natural world.' The ceremony started with sermons by leaders of the five faiths, explaining how their religious tradition could, and would, cope with the challenges of environmental degradation. These speeches were, in each case, accompanied by more evocative aspects of liturgy: Christian hymns, Buddhist chants, and Hindu temple dances. Time was also set aside for a ceremony of Repentance, where the seers asked forgiveness for harm that they or their fellow faithful had inflicted on nature.

The speakers at Assisi ranked high in the hierarchy of their faiths. They included an abbot of an ancient Buddhist shrine in north-eastern India, acting here as the personal representative of the Dalai Lama; the Minister-General of a leading Franciscan order; the Secretary-General of the Muslim World League; and the Vice-President of the World Jewish Congress. Also present were some powerful people from the secular world, such as the Italian Minister of the Environment, and Prince Philip, husband of the Queen of England and a long-time patron of the WWF. Lis Harris, covering the event for the *New Yorker*, wrote that the organizers hoped to 'communicate the conservation message of the events in Assisi to the entire global network of local priests, mullahs, rabbis, lamas, and swamis who had intimate contact with that vast segment of the population which neither read papers nor watched television nor subscribed to magazines . . .' The idea behind the ecumenical service in Assisi was thus to harness these diverse and widespread energies towards a single collective goal: the protection of the One Earth which is the abode for us all.

By the 1970s, as this book has shown, environmentalism had emerged as a worldwide movement, with its chapters and outposts in all continents. In country after country, individuals and groups made manifest their concern at the deterioration of the environment in their own village, town, district, or province. By the 1980s, however, to these local and regional problems had been added a new class of problems that could only be described as global. These included the build up of carbon dioxide and other gases in the atmosphere, the so-called greenhouse effect; the hole in the ozone layer noticed over Anatartica, caused primarily by the emissions of chlorofluorocarbons or CFCs; and the rapid decline of biological diversity through the extinction of countless species of plants, insects and animals, and sometimes of the very habitats in which they had dwelt. These were considered to be global problems in so far as the terrain where they occured was property that could be claimed by everyone or by no one. They were global also in that no nation was so fortunate as to be insulated from their effects. With regard to the change in world climate or the loss of biological diversity, there was no telling, yet, which country would suffer first or suffer most.

The sentiment that there was only one world to share, or lose, was heightened by the pictures of the earth that started coming in from outer space. On the ground the earth's expanse seemed limitless; as did its capacity to sustain an infinite increase of human appetites and demands. But from the satelite the earth suddenly appeared vulnerable and fragile: a part of the universe small in itself but with a especial resonance for those who happened to live on it. The astronaut Edgar Mitchell, who flew aboard the spaceship Apollo 14, saw the planet as 'a sparkling blue-and-white jewel' which seemed 'like a small pearl in a thick sea of black mystery.'

In the first week of 1989, the popular newsmagazine *Time* authoritatively underwrote this emergence of a global environmental consciousness. It chose the earth as the 'Planet of the Year:' this was a striking departure from its usual practice of nominating a statesman, scientist, sportsman or rock star as its 'Man of the Year.' In his lead article, Thomas A. Sancton offered a listing of the previous year's environmental disasters—dust bowls, heatwaves, floods, species gone extinct, etc.—noting that

> Everyone suddenly sensed that this gyrating globe, this precious repository of all the life that we knew of, was in danger. No single individual, no event, no movement captured imaginations or dominated headlines more than the clump of rock and soil and water and air that is our common home.

Sancton quoted several respected American scientists in support of the view that 'both the causes and effects of the [environmental] problems that threaten the earth are global, and they must be attacked globally.' He then ended with a stirring exhortation of his own:

> Every individual on the planet must be made aware of its vulnerability and of the urgent need to preserve it. No attempt to protect the environment will be successful in the long run unless ordinary people— the California housewife, the Mexican peasant, the Soviet factory worker, the Chinese farmer—are willing to adjust their life-styles. Our wasteful, careless ways must become a thing of the past. We must recycle more, procreate less, turn off lights, use mass transit, do a thousand things differently in our everyday lives. . . . Now, more than ever, the world needs leaders who can inspire their fellow citizens with a fiery sense of mission, not a nationalistic or military campaign but a universal crusade to save the planet.

II

The convention at Assisi and the *Time* story both stressed the shared interest of all peoples in combating environmental stress. The newsmagazine approvingly quoted the Missouri botanist Peter Raven: '*All* nations are tied together as to their common fate. We are all facing a common problem, which is, how are we going to keep this single resource we have, namely the world, viable?' The priests and mullahs gathered at the WWF gathering would have endorsed this statement, only substituting 'religions' for 'nations.'

Possibly the first scientists to use this image of a common earth were Barbara Ward and René Dubos, one a London-based economist, the other a New York microbiologist, who together wrote a book for the first United Nations Conference on the Human Environment, held in Stockholm in 1972. Their study was called *Only One Earth: The Care and Maintenance of a Small Planet*, and the last line of its introduction read: 'As we enter the global phase of human evolution it becomes obvious that each man has two countries, his own and the planet Earth.' This idea of a small, shared earth has provided the *raison d'etre* for the United Nations' continuing efforts to bring about international co-operation in the environmental field. In 1987, for example, it issued an influential report on sustainable development called *Our Common Future*, written by a transnational committee chaired by the Norwegian Prime Minister, Go Harlem Brundtland.

Following the Brundtland Report came the United Nations Conference on Environment and Development, known by the acronym UNCED. The UNCED was held at Rio De Janeiro in June 1992, as a somewhat delayed follow-up to the Stockholm meeting of twenty years earlier. One hundred and eighty countries participated in this 'Earth Summit;' represented in many cases by their heads of state. Alongside the official conference was held a parallel meeting of non-governmental organizations or NGOs, featuring talks and panel discussions by some of the best-known environmental activists of the globe. The Earth Summit was very likely the largest international conference ever held, and indisputably one of the most controversial. Where the spiritualists at Assisi and the scientists polled by *Time* magazine comfortably agreed on a 'common future,' the arguments at Rio suggested that while there might be one world, it was divided into two unequal halves.

The three major global problems discussed at Rio were deforestation, climate change, and the loss of biodiversity. UNCED had hoped that for each of these an inter-governmental treaty would be ratified by the participating nations. Draft treaties had already been circulated and discussed at a series of preparatory meetings in 1990 and 1991. At these 'prepcoms' two broad and generally opposing camps had emerged, whose disagreements spilled over into the discussions in June 1992. On the one side were placed the industrialized and mainly affluent countries of the North; on the other, the industrializing and mostly still-poor countries of the South.

The question of climate change emerged as the most contentious of all. To check the build up of greenhouse gases in the atmosphere, it was at first recommended that each country agree to stabilizing its carbon emissions by an agreed cut-off date, say 2015. This proposal, advanced by the Washington-based World Resources Institute (WRI), was bitterly attacked by Southern environmentalists. Anil Agarwal and Sunita Narain, of the Centre for Science and Environment, New Delhi, made a radical distinction between the 'survival emissions' of the poor and the 'luxury emissions' of the rich. They wondered how

the WRI could 'equate the carbon dioxide contributions of gas guz-
zling automobiles in Europe and North America or, for that matter,
anywhere in the Third World with the methane emissions of draught
cattle and rice fields of subsistence farmers in West Bengal or Thailand?' It was known that the oceans and forests of the globe had a
strictly limited capacity to absorb emissions, constituting as it were a
'carbon sink.' It was suggested that if there was now a dangerously
high build-up of gases incapable of absorption, then the corrective
action had first to come from the North. For if one were to allocate
equal shares of the atmosphere to all living human beings, it was apparent that the North had more than used up its share of the 'sink,'
whereas the emissions in countries like China and India were well
within the limits of the share of the sink that was rightfully theirs.

At Rio was also circulated a forest convention which sought to
strengthen global control over forest resources. Where Northern environmentalists wanted an international management regime to faci-
liate the growing of forests to serve as additional carbon sinks, their
Southern counterparts insisted that national control must rather make
way for local control, for forests were above all a community resource
providing vital inputs for the survival of millions of forest dwellers
in Asia, Africa and Latin America. A statement issued by activists
from twelve Southern countries sharply asked why, if forests needed
to be put under a system of global governance, natural resources
coveted and controlled by the North should not be subject to the
same. 'If forest management is of global consequence,' it asked, 'so is
the management of the world's oil resources. Are we going to have a
global oil convention for sustainable production, management and
conservation of the world's oil resources?'

Dispute also ranged over a proposed biodiversity treaty, thought
by Southern activists to be unduly biased in favor of Northern
biotechnology companies. The draft treaty had not allowed for just
compensation to be paid to the indigenous knowledge of local communities: knowledge that has in the past been used without payment,
or even without acknowledgement, in the development of new and
lucrative varieties of crops and medicinal drugs.

The Malaysian green activist Martin Khor Kok Peng has pointed
out that UNCED seemed unable or unwilling to face up to two central
questions: the fair assignation of responsibility for the degradation
that had already taken place, and the extent to which the United Nations and other international fora really allowed an equal voice to all
nations of the world. Many environmentalists, not all from the South,

insisted that 'all available evidence shows that the environmental crisis has been precipitated almost exclusively by the wasteful and excessive consumption in the North. Indeed, roughly 80 percent of the resources of the planet as well as its sinks are being utilized by the 20 per cent of the population that lives in Europe, North America, Oceania and Japan.' Population growth in the Third World is sometimes held to be the prime cause of environmental degradation, but as the British writer Fred Pearce asked, 'Why is it that Western environmentalists worry so much about population growth in poor countries when each new child born in North America or Europe will consume 10 or 100 times as much of the world's resources and contribute many times as much pollution? A three-child American family is, in logic, many more times as dangerous to the planet than an eight- (or even an eighty-) child African family.'

To better understand the disputes at Rio, one needs to focus as much on the components as on the extent of this consumption. A prime contributor of chlorofluorocarbons are refrigerators; a prime contributor of greenhouse gases the emissions of automobiles. The possession of a car and a fridge have come to be regarded as the index of progress, of prosperity, sometimes of civilization itself. But the truth of the matter is that virtually all Americans, Japanese, Norwegians and Belgians already own a car and a fridge, whereas most Indians, Kenyans, Colombians and Rwandans don't, but *aspire to do so in the not-so-distant future*. To ask the countries of the South to 'cap' their emissions of CFCs and CO_2 is to deny to much of humanity the hope of ever possessing well-recognized artefacts of comfort and well-being such as automobiles and refrigerators.

In this respect the California housewife and Mexican peasant certainly do not share a common past or present—on what terms can they then come to share a common future? Only in a world where their voices carry equal weight, where there is put in place a genuinely participatory democracy at the global level. But as the Centre for Science and Environment complained in a 'Statement on Global Democracy' issued specially for the Earth Summit:

> There is no effort [at present] to create new levels of power that would allow all citizens of the world to participate in global environmental management. Today, the reality is that Northern governments and institutions can, using their economic and political power, intervene in, say, Bangladesh's development. But no Bangladeshi can intervene in the development processes of Northern economies even if global warming caused largely by Northern emissions may submerge half [their] country.

III

A thoughtful account of the divisions before and during the Earth Summit has been provided by the Pakistani sociologist Tariq Banuri. Differences between North and South, he suggests, were both conflicts based on economic interests and conflicts over meanings. The same event was thus viewed very differently, 'as though people sitting in the same theatre were to be seeing two different movies.' 'Where most Northerners,' remarked Banuri—

> see UNCED as the very welcome unfolding of collective action to save humanity, many southerners, government functionaries as well as NGO activists (albeit for different reasons) fear in it the emergence of a new imperialism, of new conditionalities, and of new obstacles to the alleviation of poverty and oppression. Northerners have lined up to take part in a movie of Noah building an ark to defend us against the deluge. But the south does not seem to belong in this story; it is in a theatre on the other side of the railroad tracks, where Jesus is being crucified to save humanity, where the poor have to suffer in their poverty so that the rich can enjoy their lifestyle.

In this context, one cannot but notice a vivid contrast between the 1986 meeting of religious leaders and the meeting of nations at Rio held six years later. The first was well-meaning and consensual, but also bombastic and vague, talking platitudinously of a shared responsibility mandated by all our faiths. The second was bitter and conflictual, but also concrete and precise, estimating culpability according to extent of emissions and arguing about each country's share of the biosphere.

This book has underlined the sheer variety of environmentalism, its rich and exuberant expression over the years and across the globe. In the past, as I have suggested, there have been distinct 'national' green traditions; but these have also creatively borrowed from one another. The battles of the Earth Summit seemed to presage another kind of encounter between environmentalists, one that might be destructive and disharmonious rather than mutually beneficial.

The residues of Rio will stay with us awhile, but beyond their real and basic differences there is something that unites different kinds of environmentalists. If there is indeed an idea that unites them, which brings together America's John Muir with India's Mahatma Gandhi, Kenya's Waangari Matthai with Germany's Petra Kelly, it is, I think, the idea of *restraint*. All through history those who have commanded power have shown a conspicuous disregard of limits on their behavior, whether toward the environment or towards other humans. Capitalists have exploited workers, socialists have suppressed citizens, both have dominated nature in the belief that it cannot speak back. In their own belief, and often in their practice, Greens are marked rather by restraint: as manifest in the wonder and reverence with which the wilderness thinker looks upon the wild, or the gentleness with which the rural romantic caresses the land, or, indeed, the statistical means by which the scientific conservationist seeks to maintain nature's capital by using only the incremental growth to its stock.

A clue to what brings together all shades of green, all varieties of environmentalism, is contained also in a remark of the Indian Sinologist, Giri Deshingkar. Deshingkar once observed that modern civilization has divorced us both from the past and from the future. By undervaluing traditional knowledge and traditional institutions, it has severed our links with our forefathers and our grandmothers. At the same time, by focusing on individual achievement and the here and now, it has radically discounted the future. 'In the long run we are all dead,' claimed the British economist John Maynard Keynes, a statement that might very well be the epitaph of the twentieth century.

The philosophy of 'in the long run we are all dead' has guided economic development in the First and Third Worlds, in both socialist and capitalist countries. These processes of development have brought, in some areas and for some people, a genuine and substantial increase in human welfare. But they have also been marked by a profound insensitivity to the environment, a callous disregard for the needs of generations to come. They have also perpetuated and in some cases intensified the divisions within human society, between the consuming classes and the working classes. It is what we know as the 'global green movement' that has most insistently moved people and governments beyond this crippling shortsightedness, by struggling for a world where the tiger shall still roam the forests of the Sunderbans and the lion stalk majestically across the African plain, where the harvest of nature may be more justly distributed across the members of the human species, where our children might more freely drink the water of our rivers and breathe the air of our cities. It is in this sense that the environmental movement has shown us a common future—and the multiple paths to get to it.

Bibliographic Essay

The scholarly works on environmentalism's first wave fall neatly into two categories: histories of the origins of environmentalism in different countries and biographical studies of key figures. Among the more important national histories are, for England, Jan Marsh, *Back to the Land: The Pastoral Impulse in England, from 1800 to 1914* (London: Quartet Books, 1982), Raymond Williams, *The Country and the City* (London: Chatto and Windus, 1973); and Keith Thomas, *Man and Nature: A History of the Modern Sensibility* (New York, Pantheon, 1982); for Germany, Raymond H. Dominick III, *The Environmental Movement in Germany: Prophets and Pioneers, 1871–1971* (Bloomington: Indiana University Press, 1992); for Australia, J. M. Powell, *Environmental Management in Australia, 1788–1914* (Melbourne: Oxford University Press, 1976) and for the U.S.A., where the literature is most copious, Roderick Nash, *Wilderness and the American Mind* (third edition: New Haven: Yale University Press, 1982), Samuel P. Hays, *Conservation and the Gospel of Efficiency: The Progressive Conservation Movement, 1880 to 1920* (Cambridge: Harvard University Press, 1958), Arthur Ekirch, Jr., *Man and Nature in America* (New York: Columbia University Press, 1963); William R. Burch, Jr. *Daydreams and Nightmares: A Sociological Essay on the American Environment* (New York: Harper and Row, 1971), and Alfred Runte, *National Parks: The American Experience* (second edition: Lincoln, University of Nebraska Press, 1984).

Much of the literature has focused on specific sectors in specific countries. Thus 'national' histories of the growth of scientific forestry published in the past decade include Conrad Totman, *The Green Archipelago: Forestry in Preindustrial Japan* (1989), Nancy Peluso, *Rich Forests, Poor People: Resource Control and Resistance in Java* (1992), Madhav Gadgil and Ramachandra Guha, *This Fissured Land: An Ecological History of India* (1993)—all three books published by the University of California Press, Berkeley—and Lane Simonian,

Defending the Jaguar: A History of Conservation in Mexico (Austin: University of Texas Press, 1995). Also worthy of note is Franz Heske's *German Forestry* (New Haven: Yale University Press, 1938), a cele-bratory account of how German forest science spread all across the world.

Another sector that has attracted the attention of historians is the history of widlife conservation, following upon the popular con-cern with the decline of wild species and habitats. Africa, with its endangered populations of spectacular mammals such as the elephant and the lion, has for good reason been the favorite stomping ground of historians so inclined. Recent and well-researched studies include Raymond Bonner, *At the Hand of Man: Peril and Hope for Africa's Wildlife* (New York: Alfred Knopf, 1993), and John M. Mackenzie, *The Empire of Nature: Hunting, Conservation and British Imperial-ism* (Manchester: Manchester University Press, 1988), as well as two essay-collections, David Anderson and Richard Grove, *Conservation in Africa: People, Parks and Priorities* (Cambridge: Cambridge Univer-sity Press, 1987) and the special issue on 'The Politics of Conservation in Africa' of the *Journal of Southern African Studies* (volume 15, num-ber 2, January 1989). Keeping in mind the ecological diversity of coun-tries and continents, studies with a regional rather than national focus will form the next, or more specialized stage of research. Two such works are Mahesh Rangarajan's *Fencing the Forest: Conservation and Ecological Change in India's Central Provinces, 1860–1914* (New Delhi: Oxford University Press, 1996), and Jane Carruthers' *The Kruger National Park: A Social and Political History* (Pietermaritzburg: University of Natal Press, 1995).

Turning next to biographical studies, David Lowenthal's *George Perkins Marsh: Versatile Vermonter* (New York: Columbia University Press, 1958) stands out as an outstanding study of a great pioneering conservationist. Lowenthal's book, we may note, was published in the age of ecological innocence: he is now preparing a new edition more in tune with the temper of the times. Another thoroughly re-searched and well-written biography is Curt Meine's *Aldo Leopold: His Life and Work* (Madison: University of Wisconsin Press, 1988). John Muir completes the holy trinity of American environmentalists: and among the slew of modern works on or around Muir are Michael Cohen, *The Pathless Way: John Muir and American Wilderness* (Madi-son: University of Wisconsin Press, 1984), and Stephen Fox, *The American Conservation Movement: John Muir and His Legacy* (Madi-son: University of Wisconsin Press, 1985). There is also the valuable early study by Linnie Marsh Wolfe, *The Life of John Muir* (Madison:

University of Wisconsin Press, 1978—first published in 1945). In my analysis of Muir I have however relied directly on the prophet's writings in contemporary periodicals such as *Harper's* and *The Atlantic Monthly*, the articles through which he first alerted the public to the devastation of the American West.

Moving beyond America, the British have made the art of biography their own, as exemplified in E. P. Thompson's mammoth *William Morris: From Romantic to Revolutionary* (revised editon: London: Merlin Press, 1978) and in Jonathan Bate's much slimmer but no less provocative *Romantic Ecology: Wordsworth and the Environmental Tradition* (London: Routledge, 1991). A fine example of a 'cross-cultural' life is the Japanese scholar C. Tsuzuki's *Edward Carpenter, 1844–1929: Prophet of Human Fellowship* (Cambridge: Cambridge University Press, 1980). The environmental writings of some figures treated in Part I of this book, such as Mahatma Gandhi, J. C. Kumarappa, Patrick Geddes and Lewis Mumford, are treated at greater length in Ramachandra Guha and J. Martinez-Alier, *Varieties of Environmentalism: Essays North and South* (London: Earthscan, and New Delhi, OUP, 1997). But these writers must also be read in the original. Still valuable works include Patrick Geddes, *Cities in Evolution* (1915: reprint Williams and Norgate, 1949); J. C. Kumarappa, *The Economy of Permanence* (Wardha: All India Village Industries Associaton, 1945); Radhakamal Mukerjee, *Regional Sociology* (New York: Century Co., 1926) and *Social Ecology* (London: Longmans, Green and Co., 1942) and, especially, the two masterful ecological histories by Lewis Mumford, *Technics and Civilization* (1934) and *The Culture of Cities* (1938), both published by Harcourt, Brace and Jovanovich, New York. The American scholar Frank G. Novack Jr. has compiled a fascinating volume based on the letters between Geddes and Mumford—*Lewis Mumford and Patrick Geddes: The Correspondence* (London: Routledge, 1995).

The history of environmentalism/environmental thought in specific regions, time periods and contexts is also treated in a huge and ever-growing periodical literature. There are now two specialized journals on environmental history: the *Environmental History Review*, published in the U.S., and *Environment and History*, published in the U.K. Important essays on the subject also appear in more 'mainstream' journals such as the *American Historical Review* or the *Indian Economic and Social History Review*. Among the numerous periodical essays I have found useful let me mention only three: John Raslett, ' "Checking Nature's Desecration": Late-Victorian Environmental Organization,' in *Victorian Studies*, Winter 1983; William Beinart,

'Soil Erosion, Conservationism and Ideas about Development: a Southern African Exploration, 1900–60,' *Journal of Southern African Studies*, volume 11, number 1, 1984; and Donald Fleming, 'Roots of the New Conservation Movement,' in Donald Fleming and Bernard Bailyn, editors, *Perspectives in American History, Volume VI* (Cambridge, Mass: Charles Warren Center for Studies in American History, 1972).

Although no previous study has been so reckless as to attempt a global history of environmentalism, there is an increasing dissatisfaction with taking the nation as the framework of analysis. The links, positive and negative, between European colonial expansion and conservation are treated in Richard Grove's *Green Imperialism: Colonial Expansion, Tropical Edens and the Origins of Environmentalism* (Cambridge: Cambridge University Press, 1994), and in the essay-collection edited by Jacques Pouchepedass, *Colonisations et Environment* (Paris: Société Française d'Histoire d'Outre-Mer, 1993—orignially published as a special issue of the *Revue Française d'Histoire d' Outre-mer.*) A rich cultural history of representations of nature in the modern West is contained in Simon Schama's *Landscape and Memory* (London: HarperCollins, 1995). Another transnational study in Anna Bramwell's *Ecology in the Twentieth Century: A History* (London: Yale University Press, 1989), a comparative analysis of anti-industrial trends in Germany and Britain (despite its title, however, it is really restricted to these two countries, without a reference to Asia, Africa or Latin America and with but a few pages devoted to the U.S.).

Where works on environmentalism's first wave are generally able to maintain a critical distance from the people and processes they describe, those on the second wave are more insistently partisan, its writers influenced by events they have personally witnessed and sometimes even participated in. Nonetheless, we now have some important analyses of contemporary environmentalism that are likely to stand the test of time. Thus Philip Shabecoff's *A Fierce Green Fire: The American Environmental Movement* (New York: Hill and Wang, 1993) and Samuel P. Hays' *Beauty, Health and Permanence: The American Environmental Movement, 1955–85* (New York: Cambridge University Press, 1987), one by a journalist, the other by a veteran academic, provide authoritative analyses of a vibrant if internally divided movement. A wide-ranging anthology of writings on the wild and Deep Ecology is *The Great New Wilderness Debate* (Athens: University of Georgia Press), edited by J. Baird Callicott and Michael P. Nelsor. The struggles for 'environmental justice' are the subject of Andrew

Szasz, *EcoPopulism: Toxic Waste and the Movement for Environmental Justice* (Minneapolis: University of Minnesota Press, 1994) and Robert D. Bullard, *Dumping in Dixie: Race, Class and Environmental Quality* (Boulder: Westview Press, 1990). The British movement is well covered in Philip Lowe and Jane Goyder, *Environmental Groups in Politics* (London: Allen and Unwin, 1983), the German (or West German) movement in Werner Hülsberg, *The German Greens: A Social and Political Profile* (London: Verso, 1988), in Margit Mayer and John Ely, eds, *Between Movement and Party: The Paradox of the German Greens* (Philadelphia: Temple University Press, 1997), and in Saral Sarkar's essay 'The Green Movement in West Germany,' *Alternatives*, volume 11, number 2, 1986.

Where these are all 'national' histories, a fine comparative analysis of environmental movements in three European countries small in size but precocious in civic action is contained in Andrew Jamison, Ron Eyerman, Jacqueline Cramer and Jeppe Lessøe, *The Making of the New Environmental Consciousness: A Comparative Study of Environmental Movements in Sweden, Denmark and the Netherlands* (Edinburgh: Edinburgh University Press, 1990). Also comparative in scope is the work of Ronald Inglehart. His thesis of environmentalism as a 'postmaterialist' movement is articulated in two books: *The Silent Revolution* (1977) and *Value Change in Industrial Societies* (1990), both published by Princeton University Press.

All this is to cite books only. The periodical literature is immense: it includes two valuable special issues showcasing country studies of environmentalism, viz. *International Journal of Sociology and Social Policy*, volume 12, numbers 4–7, 1992, and *Research in Social Movements, Conflicts and Change*, Supplement 2, 1992 ('The Green Movement Worldwide'). Among the specialized English-language journals on the environment are the American periodicals *Society and Natural Resources, Whole Earth Review, Environmental Ethics* and *Capitalism, Nature, Socialism*, and the British bimonthly *The Ecologist*—all of which regularly publish essays on environmental debates and movements.

One can also expect, in the years ahead, biographies of the key thinkers and activists of modern environmentalism. Those that already exist include Barbara Wood, *Alias Papa: A Life of Fritz Schumacher* (London: Jonathan Cape, 1984), a daughter's memoir, affectionate but also informative; Frank Graham, *Since Silent Spring* (Boston: Houghton Mifflin, 1970), this a biography of a book rather than author. Well worth reading too is the autobiography of Mira Behn (Madeline Slade), *A Spirit's Pilgrimage* (London: Longman, Green and Co., 1960), the story of the encounters of a British admiral's daughter with Gandhi and village India. In a class of its own is John McPhee's *Encounters with the Archdruid: Narratives about a Conservationist and Three of His Natural Enemies* (New York: Farrar, Strauss and Giroux, 1971), a characteristically urbane and witty account of life with David Brower, ex-President of the Sierra Club, founder of Friends of the Earth, and one of America's most influential and truculent conservationists. Also a biography, but of a village rather than individual, is Michael Meyerfeld Bell's ethnographic study of how English people perceive the environment: *Childerley: Nature and Morality in an English Village* (Chicago: University of Chicago Press, 1994).

Environmentalism's second wave has also spawned a rich outcrop of polemical and exhortative works on the human predicament. Preeminent here are the works of biologists, with their unique blending of science and prophecy. Numerous books by biologists are cited in the text: one which isn't, but which is worth consulting nonetheless, is René Dubos' *A World Within: A Positive View of Mankind's Future* (London: Angus and Robertson, 1973). Next in importance are the works of philosophers who have offered acute insights into the moral and social roots of environmental abuse. One such thinker is Rudolf Bahro, a East German dissident who later played a formative role in the founding of the Green Party. See Bahro's *From Red to Green: Interviews with New Left Review* (London: Verso, 1984), and his *Building the Green Movement* (Philadelphia: New Society Publishers, 1986). The idea of 'deep ecology,' as formulated by the Norwegian philosopher Arné Naess, is discussed in Naess' *Ecology, Community, Lifestyle*, translated from the Norwegian by David Rothenberg (Cambridge: Cambridge University Press, 1986). The relevance of different religions for comprehending or solving the environmental crisis is investigated in magisterial fashion by the Iranian philosopher Seyyed Hossein Nasr in his *Religion and the Order of Nature* (Oxford: Oxford University Press, 1996). The ideas of such influential thinkers as Carson, Commoner, Ehrlich and Mumford are treated in David Macauley, ed. *Minding Nature: The Philosophers of Ecology* (New York: The Guilford Press, 1996). Finally, a thoughtful and constructive agenda for moving Western society towards a more constructive path is contained in Wolfgang Sachs, Reinhard Loske, Manfred Linz et al., *Greening the North: A Post Industrial Blueprint for Ecology and Equity* (London: Zed Books, 1998).

In comparison to its Northern counterpart, the literature on Southern environmentalism is scarce. The very idea of the 'environmentalism of the poor' runs counter to the conventional wisdom of the social sciences. While movements in defense of forest rights and against 'destructive development' were common in the India of the seventies and the Brazil of the eighties, it has taken a while for their signals to be noticed in the academy. I have therefore relied heavily on my own research and on the ongoing research of friends and colleagues. The information on Bali comes from as yet unpublished papers by Dr Carol Warren of Murdoch University, while the account of the Penan case was enabled only by my access to a forthcoming book manuscript on the subject by Dr J. Peter Brosius of the University of Georgia. An even greater debt is owed to Professor Juan Martinez-Alier of the Autonomous University of Barcelona, from whose work on Latin American environmentalism I have freely borrowed.

The published work on Southern environmentalism is limited in extent and uneven in quality. The history of Brazilian environmentalism has however been analysed in two fine articles: Karl Goldstein's essay on 'The Green Movement in Brazil,' pp. 119–93 in Matthias Finger, editor, *Research in Social Movements, Conflicts and Change, Supplement 2: The Green Movement Worldwide* (Greenwich, Conn.: Jai Press, 1992), and Eduardo J. Viola's 'The Ecologist Movement in Brazil (1974–86): from Environmentalism to Ecopolitics,' *International Journal of Urban and Regional Research*, volume 12, number 2, November 1988. Also to be noted is W. E. Hewit's essay, 'The Roman Catholic Church and Environmental Politics in Brazil,' *The Journal of the Developing Areas*, volume 26, number 1, 1992. Amazonian deforestation and Chico Mendes' struggle are discussed in Susanna Hecht and Alexander Cockburn's *The Fate of the Forest: Developers, Destroyers and Defenders of the Amazon* (London: Penguin Books, 1990). Our understanding of Brazilian environmentalism will be enriched by the publication of two book-length studies currently under preparation: one by José Augusto Padua on early (eighteenth and nineteenth century) ecological thought, the other by Margaret Keck on the contemporary environmental movement.

The Chipko movement is the subject of my book, *The Unquiet Woods: Ecological Change and Peasant Resistance in the Himalaya* (New Delhi: Oxford University Press, 1989: second revised edition, 1999), while a broader analysis of Indian environmentalism is offered in Madhav Gadgil and Ramachandra Guha, *Ecology and Equity: The Use and Abuse of Nature in Contemporary India* (London: Routledge, 1995). The relationship between women and nature is explored in

Bina Agarwal's essay, 'The Gender and Environment Debate: Lessons from India', *Feminist Studies*, volume 18, 1992. Two seminal documents are the *Citizens Reports on the Indian Environment* published by New Delhi's Centre for Science and Environment (CSE) in 1982 and 1985. Informative essays on environmental issues in South Asia are carried in the *Economic and Political Weekly*, published in Mumbai, and the monthly *Himal*, printed in Kathmandu. The history of the CSE reports mentioned above is another tribute to the internationalism of the environmental movement. The title, as well as the format (with chapters devoted to different resource sectors or particular controversies) has been emulated in the highly successful *State of the World Reports* issued annually by the Washington-based Worldwatch Institute. As it happens, the Indian reports were themselves inspired by a slim *State of the Malaysian Environment Report* brought out by the Penang group Sahabat Alam Malaysia in 1980. But despite that country's leading role in articulating the 'voice' of the South, there are no reliable books or articles on the evolution of Malaysian environmentalism. Malaysia's neighbor, Thailand, has been better served in this respect. Useful essays on environmental conflict in that country include Larry Lohmann, 'Peasants, Plantations and Pulp: the Politics of Eucalyptus in Thailand,' *Bulletin of Concerned Asian Scholars*, volume 23, number 4, 1991; Jim Taylor, 'Social Activism and Resistance on the Thai Frontier: The Case of Phra Prajak Khuttajitto,' *Bulletin of Concerned Asian Scholars*, volume 25, number 2, 1993; and Philip Hirsh, 'What are the Roots of Thai Environmentalism?,' *TEI Quarterly Environmental Journal*, volume 2, number 2, 1994. There are, as yet, no authoritative works on African environmental conflicts, but an intimate first-hand account of the Ogoni struggle can be found in Ken Saro-Wiwa's *A Month and a Day: A Detention Diary* (London: Penguin Books, 1996).

Turning now to the socialist and ex-socialist world, one must mention first of all Douglas Weiner's comprehensive history of the forgotten past of Soviet conservation, *Models of Nature: Ecology, Conservation, and Cultural Revolution in Soviet Russia* (Bloomington: Indiana University Press). There is as yet no comparable book-length study of the 'second wave' of Russian environmentalism, but insightful accounts are available in Robert G. Darst, Jr., 'Environmentalism in the USSR: the Opposition to the River Diversion Projects,' *Soviet Economy*, volume 4, number 3, 1988; and in Ze'ev Wolfson and Vladimir Butenko, 'The Green Movement in the USSR and Eastern Europe,' in Matthias Finger, editor, *Research in Social Movements,*

Conflicts and Change, Supplement 2: The Green Movement Worldwide
(Greenwich, Conn.: Jai Press, 1992).China, of course (and sadly),
has had even less experience of environmental action and environmental debate than did Soviet Russia. The one exception was the debate over the Three Gorges Dam, summarized in Dai Qing and others,
Yangtze! Yangtze, edited by Patricia Adams and John Thibodeau
(London: Earthscan, 1994).

Index